Libertine

Vega Starlight

vega@vegastarlight.com

ISBN 979-8-9951196-3-0

Any resemblance to real persons,
either living or dead,
is purely intentional.

There is no such thing as a moral or immoral book.

~ Oscar Wilde

LIBERTINE

No Strings

Elegy

Walking through a graveyard.
An old graveyard.
But also new.
Tombstones.
Old and new.
Long forgotten under the hedges,
here is what I found:
"No Strings"
The antithesis of remembrance.
A nameless stone.
Lonely.
Only "No Strings"
How many generations must pass before we are forgotten?
Hedges tangle and corrupt the only remaining record of life.
A loved person,
even without strings,
would surely not be forgotten so quickly, right?
It is impossible to die in the manner which we most desire.
The irony of “No Strings” is:
A headstone, a plot, a beautiful cathedral.
These are not the final wishes of the destitute.
Can there truly be “No Strings"?
Between the life and death of a person,
with such an extravagant funeral?
Such an upscale graveyard?
Death does not cut the strings of the wealthy.
If you want "No Strings"
give your money to the destitute.
Erase yourself.

Erase every word you ever wrote.
Every pen stroke.
Go away.
Far, far away.
Prepare the boat.
Sail away from port.
Far, far away.
Drown your sorrows.
Drown yourself in the ocean.
Faster, faster.
Deeper, deeper.
No concerns of food or water.
This is a one-way trip.
Give your money away.
Just go far, far, far, far away.
Sail away from memories.
Away from everyone you know.
Away from anyone who might remember you.
When you reach your watery grave,
your whirlpool of nothingness.
Jump, dear sailor.
Man overboard!
Feckless slug overboard.
Cut your strings.
Burn your bridges.
Empty your wallet.
"No Strings."

Perhaps Thetis will collect you.

Of Ashes and Stitches

Lamentation

Cinderella,
Sweep the ashes.
Bring the sutures,
Stitch my slashes.

Bijoux

Epistolary

What Happened?
Who knows?
Fate.
Together.
Apart.
Fate strikes.
Once, twice...thrice?
Our eyes met,
our hearts met,
yet we fell apart.
Why?
Who knows?
Watching, studying.
A jewel bound.
But not to me.
Unbound.
Leased?
Or owned?
By another.
Jealousy!
But why?
What difference does it make?
We fell apart.
Or...did we?
Yes, we fell apart.
Time passes.
So much time.
Are you happy?
My jewel, bijoux?

Who knows?
Did you think of me?
Wait, I will ask a better question:
Do you remember me?
I remember you.
Are such thoughts relevant?
Shock and awe; war campaign; blood war; blood diamond.
Campaign to see a jewel with my own eyes.
Emerald.
Green.
Envy.
Jealousy.
You enter the room.
But time...
...so much time has passed since we last spoke.
And pain?
Are you in pain?
Do these things matter?
What is real?
Jealousy?
Who knows?
You ignore me.
I should ignore you, also.
Risk.
Take the risk.
Talk to her.
Crown Jewel.
Talk to her.
Bijoux?
You laughed at me.
Laughed.
In my mind, nothing has changed.
In your mind, everything has changed.
Laughed.

Memories clash.
I wanted you closer,
yet you felt pushed away.
We fell apart, but why?
Who knows?
Certainly, I do not know.
Liar.
I am a liar.
I ended it.
This relationship fell apart because I ended it.
And now you laugh at me.
Your pain is palpable.
No, I misunderstood.
The pain is mine.
I misspoke.
A heart full of emotion.
Could I have a place?
Amongst such pain?
A place in my own heart?
There is no room in here.
Do such thoughts matter?
I can't get a thought in edge ways.
Do you remember me?
Who knows?
I surely do not.
Will we be friends?
Lovers?
Haters?
Nothing?
You laughed because we are nothing.
I made us nothing.
Nothing.
I am nothing.
And you laugh.

Will we be a team?
Hand in hand.
Repelling the evils of the world.
Who knows?
I know.
Nothing.
Just laughter.
Secrets of the heart.
Growth.
Pain.
Growth and pain.
Just pain.
Growing pains.
Lonely.
Lonely but not alone.
Liar.
Alone.
Regression.
Progression?
Regression.
Remission.
Getting over me.
Who knows?
I no longer do.
Liar.
I know.
Nothing.
My Crown Jewel.
Bijoux.
What are you?
What am I?
What are we?
Lost in nothing.
Where are you?

Who knows?
Liar.
I know where you are.
Where you are not.
Not with me.

I wish you would stop laughing.

Cold Bricks

Free Verse

Ice rains down,
the world glazes over.
Fire warms hearth and heart.
My thoughts drift to spring clover.
Purple little clouds.
The night is darkest
when light is lowest.
Awake in the cold
when the fire slowest.
The clover dreams retreat
leaving a bleak, winter depression.
Brown, dormant, crunchy, brittle.

Another therapist?
Another session?

Icicles slip,
pierce the soil.
Hearth is home but heart is wounded.

Cold bricks and turmoil.

Immortal

Free Verse

The greatest legacy of mankind?
Death.
War.
Disaster.
Why?
Because we chase immortality.
It cannot be avoided.
Deny not, dear reader.
You also seek immortality.
Not a ceasing heartbeat.
Living in the beating heart
of those we leave behind.
Living in their minds.
To live in the minds of countless generations,
whom we have no chance of saluting.
Moses or Shakespeare?
Joshua or Dante?
Who is Godliest?
Who is Immortal?
Immortality is not derived from money,
fame,
popularity,
property,
success,
nor inheritance.
Only art is immortal;
however, art is subjective and
art fades.
Trends,

ideas,
mediums,
politics,
anger,
happiness,
phases,
beliefs,
clicks,
and styles.
They come and go.
But art is permanent.
Ink is permanent.
The written word is immortal.
The story of art is not a universal truth.
Immortality is not subjective.
Immortality is objective.
Here, let me hold your hand and show you
the objectively universal truth of humanity:
only the heart is immortal.
Beating or long buried,
it matters not.
A warrior's pulsing heart,
spills blood upon the ground.
A fountain pen,
spills ink upon the parchment.
Words bind humanity together.
Words are timeless.
Who is remembered?
Who is immortal?
The warrior or the scribe?

The humble pen:
sword of the immortal heart.

Matador

Free Verse

The Matador.
Surgical precision.
Piercing strikes.
The tip of the spear is not enough
to deliver death. Just as one feather
cannot fly.
One thousand cuts
brings the bull to his knees.
The ink in my heart
is a slave to my pen.
One thousand paper cuts.
A lover's glancing blows.
Passive aggressive bitch.
Blood and ink
spills and splatters.

The reg flag waves, unfurled in victory.

White Silence

Free Verse

Like a fresh snowfall,
so the blank page.
Soft, empty, undisturbed.
A faint crunch, a delicate rustle.
One step, one turn.
Gentle breeze flutters the white
page. Inhale the clean
air infused with moldy musk.
Ancient ink,
long turned acidic.

Come play!
Let's build a snowman!

Crumpled ideas
balled and stacked
on upon another
in the trash bin.

But be warned, brave soul.
Neither snow nor the blank page
will forgive your trespasses.

Footprints and ink betray you.

Black Noise

Free Verse

There is only darkness.
A vastness
devoid of light.
A blight
upon what is bright.
A plague
upon what is virginal.
A blackness
upon what is hominal.
Sulfur stifles sinuses.
Sniffing, scathing sinuses.
Scorching orange dawn.
The Morning Star falls.
The screams are agonizing and relentless:
Dante's sins and sinners.
What is a music note upon a page?
Black checks white.
Checkmate.
White always falls to black.
Surrenders its silence.
Surrenders in silence.
Unless it is torn.
Black is potential.
Black is noise.
Scream these words:
Ink shatters delicate parchment.
Like a champagne glass
resonating harmoniously with the chaos of symphony.
Silence is shattered.

Reverberating through the void of cavernous nothing.
Black pierces white.

The breath of one-thousand golden trumpets.

Alone

Free Verse

Born alone, die alone.
That's what *they* say.
They. Who are *they*?
I guess *they* would know.
Is *they* self-aware?
And in-between, what?
I'll tell you what.

Alone.

They forget to tell you that part.
Between life and death,
beginning and end,
we must bind our own wounds,
bandage our own cuts,
set our own broken bones,
mend our own broken hearts.

Maybe *they* don't know,
they who say.
Start and stop alone.
They are never alone.
They fear alone,
just as *they* fear life and death.
They will never know themselves.

Fear surrounds *they* with:

family, spouses, friends, associates, offspring, pets, acquaintances,
bosses, coworkers, neighbors, relatives, cousins, uncles, aunts, teachers, lovers,
mothers, mistresses, studs, that mysterious other.

They know nothing of alone.
But *they* know fear.

Heal your own flaws.
Bleed not your worrisome heart.

There is glory and valiance in loneliness.

To Dream is To Lie

Poet's Prose

I died yesterday.

I know this to be true because I felt the bullet pass through my skull.

Spare me your pity - it was an easy decision.

My life has been a joke for years, and it was only a matter of time before it ended. I knew my life would end in an anti-climactic withering of weakness and depression.

People are calling it tragic, but is that the truth?

"Normal" life has a way of masking truths and lies.

Shit, shower, dress, eat, drive, work, drive, eat, drink, undress, fuck, sleep.
Shit, shower, dress, eat, drive, work, drive, eat, drink, undress, fuck, sleep.
Shit, shower, dress, eat, drive, work, drive, eat, drink, undress, fuck, sleep.

Wash, rinse, repeat.

What is truth and what is lie?

Life has ended when this question is no longer able to be answered.

Alive outside, dead inside.

The only truth is that I have been wallowing in lies for years.
I am unable to distinguish between what is dream and what is reality.

Perhaps you have felt this same hazy confusion about the world.

In the confusion and uncertainty of waking from a particularly sinister nightmare, we are given a moment of clarity before thrust violently back into the conscious reality of our meaninglessly mundane lives.

As the eyes open, the mind grasps at straws; searching desperately for a sober recollection of the day before.

The body is gripped by anxiety as the lie of the dream crashes into the truth of reality.

In this brief moment of being between dream and reality, there is only fear.

The fear survives only for the blink of an eye.

The fear of my terrible actions in dreams becoming the truth in reality.

My entire waking life has become this fear – a complete disassociation of lie and truth, of dream and reality, of falseness and memory, of paranoia and rationality.

I am alone now.

I am surrounded by nothing.

Numb to all lies.
Numb to all truths.

There is only blackness.

Do not pity me, for no others shall.

There is only blackness here. In this place, there is no one left for me to hurt.

This is where I deserve to be.

I wrapped my lips around the barrel of a gun and put a bullet in my head. I know this is the truth because I no longer feel fear.

No longer am I stuck in that moment between nightmare and waking.

There is only blackness.

This is for the best.

Waking Up Angry

Poet's Prose

To wake up angry is the greatest peril!

We humans are capable creatures who are able to overcome gargantuan problems, but waking up angry cannot be avoided.

There are justifiable circumstances for a person to wake up angry.

Nightmares, a snoring partner, a creaking house, or a farting dog are all worthy of annoyance.

Although these reasons for anger can be justified, it should be recognized that anger is an involuntary emotion.

Everyone feels anger and the emotion should not be ignored.

Waking up angry is not a choice.
Waking up angry is not your fault;
however, the manner in which you choose to react to anger is your responsibility, and you alone shoulder the consequences of your words and actions.

Let us examine the three phases of anger:

The first phase is provocation.
Provocation is the reason for being angry.

Waking up angry is not a choice.
Waking up angry is not your fault.
Waking up angry is a standalone provocation.

The second phase is reaction.
How will you choose to deal with the anger?

Reacting to anger is your fault and is deserving of consequences. The people around you do not deserve to experience your reaction to anger, regardless that the initial provocation is not your fault.

The third phase is harboring.
How long will you choose to feel angry?

Harboring anger is also a choice and is deserving of consequences. Harboring anger allows it to live in your mind without paying any rent.

Do not feel guilty about being provoked into anger.

You do not have a choice in waking up angry;
however, you do have a choice in how you deal with the anger.

Ultimately, if you choose reaction and harboring, your actions will likely hurt you more than the person you intended to hurt.

Issues

Ode

I knew she had issues.
I loved her anyways.

Wash, rinse, repeat.

Crazy

Free Verse

Crazy people lack credibility.
Crazy people are cut
off from the demands and expectations
that made them crazy to begin with.
Naked.
They have nothing more to lose.
Free.
The most dangerous person
is the person with nothing to lose.

Strip naked, dear reader.

Jealous

Shakespearean Sonnet

Infected soul doth rot a putrid green.
Dark side, vile side, indicted vanity.
A pedestal upon which sits my queen.
My fate is tied to toxic liberty.

From simple words, rising thunderheads brood.
Gashes, slashes, forlorn hemorrhaged heart.
Her innocent moves amp my rancid mood.
In flesh my buried fangs shall never part.

A fling then ring, wedding and honeymoon.
Maintain altitude, wing is doomed to stall.
Rank gulag chains I must escape from soon.
Desert the girl before her rage, the squall.

A life of strife, I surely guarantee.
A child and wife, this path is not for me.

Dancing

Lamentation

Dancing in the dark.
No one can see my scars.

Please, don't touch me.

Lonely

Ballad

There is a type of lonely
few of us know.
Those with conscience
understand such woes.

My loneliness is self-inflicted;
left over when I mourn.
A thousand bolts of anger;
my paranoia, a raging storm.

My phone calls ignored;
all the empty promises.
Trust built then shattered;
love is our token nemesis.

Those of us with conscience
are lonely because we know
we deserve better treatment
from those we care for so.

Best Friend

Epistolary

What do you do when,
Your best friend does not care?
Around the circle we go again,
Down another flight of stairs.
How long should I maintain,
A one-sided friendship?
A sickly, straining frame,
Crushed beneath its weight.
This show has worn me down,
But I hide the pain as best I can.
Losing my best friend is not affecting me,
Liar - you can barely stand.
Holding on for the sake of others,
For the sake of fake.
No, I do not mean the friend.
The children, the family, the mutual friends.
How long must I pretend for these people?
There is only one way this can go,
Only one way I can grow.
I am the villain.
I am the one causing problems.
I am to blame.
It is the only logical solution.
A best friend would never be such,
A stain on glass like pollution.
Beautiful stained glass.
Smashed.
Right?
Right.

What do you do when,
Your best friend looks into your eyes.
Into your eyes and lies?
Tells you that they have made mistakes.
Tells you that they will change.
Tells you things will get better.
Tells you they love you.
And then nothing.
Nothing!
Return to the same old same old routine.
Have you ever felt tolerated?
Made to feel obscene?
Even when you cooperated?
A second-class citizen.
Marginalized.
Denizen of nothing.
Why?
Because success eludes you?
No.
Because success means different things to you.
True success is self-discovery.
Oh, but not for the best friend.
Success means nothing more than money,
Defined by overspend.
Soul, heart, passion, intellect, pursuits,
Music, art, dreams, literature, nature, faith.
They mean nothing to the narcissist.
They mean nothing to the best friend.
No calls.
No texts.
No emails.
Have you ever been delegated?
My best friend delegates.
You have made it clear that I am disliked,

Why further insult me with delegation?
Treating me like an obligation?
Like an employee?
I am not your employee.
There is nothing more insulting,
than being looked down upon by a best friend.
A best friend should be equal.
An equal relationship,
Bring something to the table.
He judges a person's worth,
By how much money they make.
Not by accomplishments or intellect,
I really must eject.
I am exhausted,
I cannot continue.
I no longer fear the consequences,
Of slicing though the sinew.
I shed the fake and the false.
I reject the status quo.
To hell with what people think.
I know the truth.
My best friend hides.
He hides himself.
But I know the truth.
Insecure, narcissistic, shallow, passionless, medicated.
Fake.
An empire built on medication and therapy.
A family built with amphetamines and secularism.

To my best friend:
I tried.
I wish you the best, but I give up.

Goodbye.

Sophia

Epistolary

Do not bring old baggage to a new relationship.
That is common advice, right?
How much time is needed
before old baggage dissipates?
Dissolve into the day to day.
Just another lover.
Every lover is different, as *they* say.
Every relationship is different, as *they* say.
They.
Always *they*.
One day, I would like to have a chat with *they*.
They have some explaining to do.
But I digress.
Four years.
Perhaps five.
A brutal, abusive, scarring relationship.
Five years.
Do not misunderstand.
I do not proclaim that after five years,
a person must get over their pain.
No.
I simply mean that after five years,
pain becomes manageable enough to love someone new.
Someone new.
How long we have waited for this day.
Yes, we.
I said we.
Why? I don't know.
Every mistake is a new me, an old me.

Every relationship.
Every failure.
So many me and we.
Broken, smashed, stuffed inside of me.
Someone new.
Sophia!
So fresh, so new, so supple, so ready.
Sophie, Soph, So,Sophia, Mamamia.
What beautiful children you could make.
Just one seed is all it would take.
One chance and a seed.
Locked, bound, leashed, chained, restricted,
in love with me forever.
One seed is all it would take.
Have you ever assigned nicknames
to a person who is unaware of your existence?
Sophia, Maria, Magdalena, Sarina, Falina, Halina, Katrina, Mamacita.
They say when a person likes you as more than a friend,
they find a way to be around you.
Even if you do not know each other.
Again, they.
We really must track down this they.
I made myself known to Sophia.
Spent time around her.
Her slender, straight fingers working the espresso machine.
I wake up to Sophia.
Every. Single. Day.
Not literally, of course.
But she does wake me up every day.
Not only with coffee,
but with smiles, teeth, kind words, swaying hair, bouncing steps.
Sophia's vibrancy is like a flower growing from mud.
The blackness, the bleakness, the pain of my life.
And somehow, Sophia manages to flourish in my heart.

Weeks of this pass.
Then...she notices me.
Something changes.
Have you ever experienced this magic moment?
When you are noticed by someone who previously
was blissfully unaware that you breathe, lust, yearn, dream.
She noticed.
She did more than notice.
She engaged.
"Have a great day."
She wrote this message to me.
A pen and paper.
Wrote a message to me.
Don't be confused; it was girlfriend Sophia, not barista Sophia.
Do you have trophies on your wall?
Souvenirs on your mantle?
Magnets on your refrigerator?
Small reminders of happy moments.
I do, too.
"Have a great day."
A priceless artifact.
And it is an artifact.
Do you know why?
I think you know why.
It is an artifact because this is not a happy story.
There is no happy ending for a person filled with:
Pain, regret, fear, guilt, doubt, loathing, grease, dirt.
Have you ever held something valuable?
Something impossibly valuable?
And then it disappears?
Like walking along the beach.
A diamond amongst billions of grains of sand.
A diamond glistens in your eye.
Pick it from the sand, hold it, cherish it.

Before you can put the diamond away safely in your pocket,
a wave.
You forgot about the waves,
While you were enraptured by the diamond.
The wave of blackness.
Forgot about the ocean.
Swell after swell pounds you back into coherence.
The drunkenness of Sophia is washed away.
One wave at a time.
Deposited in the backwash,
gulping for air,
slashed by shells,
skin rubbed raw by sand.
But I assure you, my friend.
(Are you my friend? Probably not, but I digress.)
Another wave smacks you.
Hard.
The diamond is gone.
You can scrounge around.
Swim in the surf.
Sift the sand.
But the diamond is gone.
We had a great conversation.
I was convinced that I had finally found my wife.
Gorgeous, youthful, vibrant, faithful, musical.
Did I mention that she plays piano and sings?
Please!
I will faint if I discuss her anymore!
You see, she is moving away in a week.
Moving away to pursue her dreams.
It is not the dream of a diamond to be possessed.
A diamond must be among its own.
A diamond must be passed along from one gracious hand to the next.
Glitter.

Shine.
Hope.
Future.
What I bring is death.
Death of the future.
Death of optimism.
Infatuation.
Jealousy.
Shadow.
Rank and dank and meek and reek.
Sophia has God in her heart.
Sophia soars with Michael at the Right Hand.
I pray that God sees the regret in my heart
and judges me as more than the serpent of the Left.
I wish not to be with Samael.
Have I made a covenant with Samael?
Could we have been something?
Sophia in love with a gutter-groveling poet?
A poet darkly?
In time, I could have convinced her.
Manipulated her.
Like I have done so many times before.
Is a shattered diamond still a diamond?
Dust does not glimmer, shimmer, shine.
No.
A shattered diamond is no better than sand.
Sand through the sieve.
I will repent alone.
I will grovel alone.
Grovel, wallow, hollow,
in the hovel of my old baggage.
I would have a chat with they.
And tell they that five years was not enough.
The old baggage,

around my neck.
Can a Master wear a collar?
Oh, yes.
The collar of regret bears a leash that is locked permanently.
Inescapable.

"Have a great day."
Have a great life.
Have a great life, Sophia.

I am glad that you saved yourself
from becoming my wife.

Dichotomy

Dialog

Hi.
Hello.

It's nice to meet you.
We have talked for countless hours in the past.

Oh, I vaguely recall.
Good to know that I was memorable.

My boyfriend couldn't come tonight.
What a lovely topic. Tell me more.

I'm not supposed to be talking to anyone.
Lucky me.

What do you like to do?
Fall for girls who couldn't care less.

Am I one of those?
Yep.

I don't think I am one of those.
You are.

We were not on the same page before.
So, you do remember dating me.

I wouldn't call it dating.
Oh?

I don't write people off quickly.
You forgot about me rather quickly.

Do you mind if I hug you?
Sure.

My boyfriend is a great guy. You would like him. We have known each other for nine years but only as of recent did we become serious. It has been great so far. I'm really happy. Actually, he bought me this dress. Do you like it? He is taking me shopping again tomorrow. He wants to find some lingerie outfits for me to wear next weekend. We are going on vacation and staying at an amazing resort. I know we haven't been dating long but I can't help to imagine us as married.

That was quite a monologue.

I just want to say that you look really handsome.
I'm flattered.

Could you excuse me for a moment?
That's fine.

Sorry to interrupt. I had a phone call.
Who was it?

It was my boyfriend. Why do you care who called?
It was an innocent question.

I like you, but I think this is not a healthy conversation.
You have been telling me for two years that you like me.

Two years?
Yes, we met you two years ago.

Oh well. Regardless, I don't like your aggressive criticism.
Aggressive criticism of what?

The things you say are criticisms.
That's news to me.

You should think about our conversation.
I'll get right on that.

You are rude. I'm going home. If you give me your number, I will call you when I get home.
You deleted my number. Imagine that.

May I ask you something?
Ask me anything.

Would you have preferred if I said nothing to you tonight?
I would prefer to be more. I like you and I want to be more. That is my preference.

Maybe we can get together tomorrow after my boyfriend leaves for work.
That's not what I meant.

On Greatness

Free Verse

I know something about you, not even having known you.

I know that you have greatness within your soul.

You have the ability to do things you cannot imagine.

You have talents and skills for which you have not yet reached.

Gaze into the mirror;
admit to yourself that you have put forth your best effort.

Unless you attempt to do something
beyond
that which you have already mastered,
you will never grow.

Design a goal that will make you stretch.

What is it you desired in the past but decided could not be accomplished?

Revive the desire.

When you pursue a goal outside of your comfort zone,
you will discover new talents and abilities.

If you continue to avoid pursuing your goals, you will commit spiritual suicide.
Alive but dead inside.
You may as well be six feet under.

Remember this, dear reader:
Practice does not make perfect.
Practice makes improvement.
Perfection does not exist.

You can always better your best.
You have not yet done your best work.

Trash

Epistolary

I came upon a piece of trash in a parking lot.
Yellow paper, legal pad paper, waylaid.
Used, abused, balled into cannon fodder.

Lane,
It has been great
walking with you. I
wish all the luck
at your new job.
They are lucky
to have you.

(Someone) loves Lane.
Lane does not love (someone).
Lane tried to let (someone) down easy.
A new job.
An excuse to escape the relationship.
(Someone) was hurt but not deterred.
(Someone) left a note on Lane's car.
Lane left work for the last time from this building.
Lane found the note under the windshield wiper.
Just as Lane discarded the job in favor of a new one,
the love note was also discarded.
It was no longer a love note.
It became trash.
Another victim in the wake of Lane's selfish decisions.
(Someone) needs to move on.

Morning Star

Shakespearean Sonnet

The fateful day did come when Heaven cleaved.
For Yahweh's throne, Lucifer sang reveille.
His sycophants rallied with arms to heed.
The Vain One's call to march on God, belayed.

Creator of the stars and moons, forsake.
My strength imbues this flock, a new council.
To build what Yahweh only dreamed to make.
On wings of death, I shall impale and kill.

Right hand of God shatters into bright light.
His scale of justice weighted towards Holy.
The sword of Michael falls upon the flock.
Through Heaven's clouds, the sky, the earth, a folly.

The Morning Star, Lucifer, fell to Hell.
Banished by Michael, a story God will tell.

Walking Away from Rainbows

Free Verse Tercets

I woke up this morning.
I felt ill.
I almost always feel ill these days.

Feeling ill puts me in a bad mood.
An eye for an eye.
I try my best, I really do.

Autumn mornings are a special gift.
Calm, cool, foggy, cloudy.
The only sounds are the birds not strong enough to migrate.

There is a beautiful rainbow.
Piercing through pink cotton ball clouds.
A rainbow just for me.

I smile upwards and take solace in the rainbow.
I vow to be cheerful despite feeling ill.
I gaze at the rainbow and get lost in my thoughts.

Screaming.
Silence shatters.
Serene breaks.

The tea pot; shrieking.
Destroys my three second relationship with the rainbow.
I am a professional at short term relationships.

Back to the mundane.

Back to the recovery.
Back to the grind.

Despite my best efforts and intentions,
My previous decisions always have a way of halting the present.
I want to stop walking away from rainbows.

Indifference

Free Verse

Love me, leave me, hate me.
Emotional prison.
Flip a coin.
Call a side.
Heads.
Love and hate.
Two sides of the same coin.
Heads roll.
Emotional poison.
Escape your sentence.
Cheat your death.
The jailer's key is within reach.
The antidote drips-drips-drips intravenous.

Indifference is the only release.

Zero Sum Game

Ballad

I'm in love with a girl.
She doesn't know my name.
La flaka? La gorda!
Our humor, much the same.

Long blond hair.
Fat breasts.
And hips to match!
The things I would do if pressed.

Another single mom.
I'll destroy her life.
Or will she destroy mine?
Mutually assured strife.

No, this time I will hide.
Daydreaming of indivisible.
No, I learned my lesson last time.
It is better to remain invisible.

So I told myself,
but I never listen.
If she flirts with me, I'll ask her out.
Oh, how her lips glisten.

Oh my God, you are so handsome.
My name is Britney.
Thanks. Let's go on a date.
Sorry. You can't be with me.

I lose.

Again.

Repent

Free Verse

I do not know why I am here.
But I tell you this:
take me away.
In all that there is,
in everything,
do this:
tonight!
Do this tonight:
go outside and look up.
Tell me I deserve to be here.
Tell me that you deserve to be here, too.
Liar.
You and I are nothing in the vastness of everything.
Humble yourself.

Lower your expectations.
Adjust your morality.

Bury Me

Lamentation

Please.
Get me out of here.
Let me join you.

I can't do this on my own.

Mirror Mirror

Free Verse

Mirror, Mirror
on the wall.
Who's the fairest
of them all?

If not for society's judgments,
I would not own a mirror.

The excruciating minutia
of vigilantly maintaining
my aging exterior
is taking a toll.

My mind is on auto-draft.
Pay the toll.
Pay the Boat Man.
What difference does it make to me at this point?

How strange to gaze at the body,
it blunts and dulls with time.
While the mind hones and sharpens,
more lethal by the day.

Sugar Pie

Dialog

I always liked your style.
Silent and remissive.

I miss You.

But you don't realize the evil of your actions.
Maybe we can be friends.
Strip away the intensity.

Why?

Because I don't trust you anymore.

I will try harder.

Then become weaker.
More desperate.

I cannot be less.
I cannot be worse.
I have reached the bottom of the well.
Wet and dank.

Then dig deeper.
Black and bleak.
Owned.
Controlled.
Nothing.

Nothing.

Say no more.
I need you to be more stable.
Do you understand?
Less impetus.

You don't even like me.

Nor does anyone else.

You will never leave Pixie.

Do you wish I had never met Pixie?

Does Pixie know that we still talk?

Do you wish I had never met Pixie?

I don't want to be a secret anymore.

Do you wish I had never met Pixie?

I wish only for Your happiness.

Goodbye, Vega.
...why are you on the floor?

Tiffany

Dialog

Hello, Tiffany.
How are you today?

I'm not sure.
I was just going where the day led,
and it's been really fun so far.

If you had one sentence
to say to the person you love most in the world
before you die, what would you say?

I would tell them that I love them.
Not really very original,
but it's probably what I would do.

Good.
Honesty is a virtuous imperative.
What do you value above all else?

Happiness.

That is cheating.
What makes you happiest?

Honestly, I don't know.
I've been trying to figure that out lately.

Why do you get out of bed?

Boredom.
If I laid in bed all day, I wouldn't be doing more than existing.
The only thing that makes me happy is trying new ~~things~~ [people].

Goodbye, Tiffany.

The Rankle and File

Political

The rankle and file.
Marching in line to their own beat.
Left.
Left.
Left, blight, left.

The Path Narrows

Ballad with Refrain

A baby is born into a flowering meadow.
Gentle winds tease dancing leaves.
Bursting flowers put on a show.
Ignorant and unaware of the bereaved.

The path narrows.

Weaned from the breast.
Lacking words to express emotions.
Separation anxiety and unrest.
Medicines and potions.

The path narrows.

Walking is good.
Falling is bad.
Choosing a mood.
Why are you sad?

The path narrows.

First day of school.
Will they one day be President?
Don't be a fool.
Coddled and hesitant.

The path narrows.

Childhood diseases.

Vaccine injuries.
Chickenpox, pneumonia, measles.
Comply or be shunned from society.

The path narrows.

Playground fights.
A stolen girlfriend.
Past your bedtime, turn out the lights.
A last desperate text, push send.

The path narrows.

Driver license.
Near miss, near miss.
Tensions heighten.
Mother's hiss.

The path narrows.

The invincible child.
Also known as young adult.
Zero consequences, be wild.
Choices have consequences, tumult.

The path narrows.

Time smothers.
Years strangle.
Friends are gone, can't find others.
Slave to society, career is a bangle.

The path narrows.

Blink once and you are old.
One thousand diseases.
Mortgage a cure, wherever medicines are sold!
The doctor will see you when she pleases.

The path narrows.

Blink twice and see a sickle.
Death has come, see the mice?
IV, heart monitor, stitches - life is fickle.
Hell is a broiler, smell the spice.

The path narrows.

World.
Road.
Tight rope.
Sickle blade.

The path ends.

Black Orchid

Epistolary

I feel your:

expectations
frustration
insecurity

I feel your:

exhaustion
resignation
fear
lies you tell yourself
lies you tell me
confusion
searching
wondering
brooding
abandonment
anger
body count
inability
inaction
camouflage
single mother desolation
baby daddy drama
motherly instincts shattered
dependence upon the past
lovers, so many lovers
(not lovers, just pump and dump Chads)

violence
laziness
indecisiveness, thinly veiled
bad decisions
broken spirit
desperation
respiration
delusion
tongue licking attention from a knife
failure
fatherless vibes

Twinkle Twinkle

Blackout

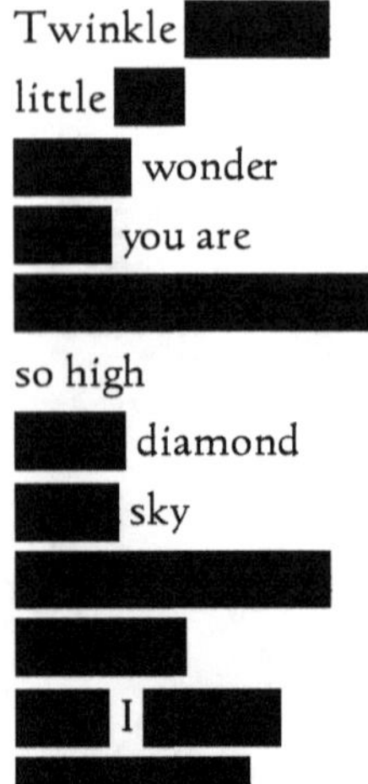

Twinkle
little
wonder
you are

so high
diamond
sky

I

Cancel Culture

Free Verse

Relationships do not come easily for me.
I work tirelessly.
Days, weeks, months.
It drains me to the bone.
Working around the clock.
To make friends while suppressing my demons.
It is difficult work.
Back breaking labor.
Knuckles ground to the bone.
A war on two fronts.
Two theaters.
Two stages.
Two main characters.
Two fictions.
In an instant, a single moment.
Everything I have built vanishes.
One incident.
Months of being a feckless slug.
I conjure a spine and stand up for myself.
Other people stand up for themselves every day.
Yet they have many friends.
I stand up for myself once.
All the friendships go away.
I am told that I am a terrible person with a terrible reputation.
No one has my back.
Because I stood up for myself.
Once.

People only like me when I am meaningless.

Cabin Fever

Free Verse

There is nothing worse than not being able to do something.

Something.
Some-thing.
Some   thing.
Some.
Thing.

Or anything, for that matter.

Snow falls wet and heavy.
The wind whips and lashes.
The door is frozen shut.
Entombed.
Snow drift.
Smoke rises from the fireplace.
Leaving the chimney.
Ripped into a wild torrent of snow devils.
Tiny tornadoes of snow climb and climb.
Then gone.
Snow blows sideways and erases the snow devils.
Life is good.
A hot shower.
Firewood stacked high.
The dog laid out on the hot hearth.
Plenty of food on the stove.
But the blizzard.
Stay inside.
Cuddle by the flames.

Heat of flames.
Heat of passion.
Heat of friction.
Skin on skin.
Fluid in fluid.
Read a book.
Sip a steaming coffee.
Sure, it is fun.
At first.
For a while.
But how many hours can this continue?
How many days could you endure?
Cabin fever.
Cabin fever?
No.
Not for me.
Cabin fever is for healthy people.
Sick people do not experience cabin fever.
People who have survived death do not get cabin fever.
Smash the door.
Break the seal.
Wake the dead.
Rise.
Go outside.
Feel the cold.
Am I still alive?
I feel the frigid cold.
The Winter Queen.
Her sword on my shoulder, knighted.
Prince of Cold.
I stand in the snow.
The blizzard tears at my face.
No jacket, no hat.
Just a shirt and my camera.

Soaking wet lens.
My hair twirls about.
Face flushing hot.
Wet snow pierces my skin.
One thousand Novocain injections.
A hospital bed or a blizzard?
What would you choose?
Give me the blizzard.
Give me the blizzard until I shiver, and ache, and hate, and love.
Give me the blizzard until it hurts so badly that I feel life.
So badly that I fear Death.
Feel it down to my bones.
His scythe slashes deep.
The cold and painful reality of no longer being in a hospital bed.
But somehow.
The hospital bed is colder.
More painful.
More deadly.
No.
Give me winter.
Give me entombed.

Cabin fever is for healthy people.

Blackbirds (Mind the Hawk)

Haibun

The blackbirds hail from the west. Over the trees and into the field they pour. Cascading like the torrent of a storm swollen waterfall. The voluble blackbirds harmonize. Millions of songs and chirps each moment. In the same moment, millions of wings beat the air. A drumming so rapid that it is a singular hum. Black wings. Red wings. Brown wings. White wings. A stream of hungry vagabonds crashing down from the frigid winter sky. A fire hose of black noise. A black cloud of wings. Opaque. Black as spilled ink. Black as the night sky against clear, brilliant blue. Blackbirds fall upon the the freshly harvested fields. Corn to fill the bellies of the homeless. One bird alights, the next lands just a bit further, and the next just a bit further, and the next just a bit further. When the corn has been devoured, it is the first bird to alight who now finds themselves in the rear of the flock. It takes to the sky and moves to the front of the flock. It alights on unmolested corn. Then the next bird, who is now in the rear, follows the first and lands in front - the next just a bit further, and the next just a bit further. In this rolling, sequential leapfrogging, the blackbirds are a wave. A black wave as ominous as a tsunami. Countless and endless, rolling and cresting waves upon a cerulean sea. Cresting, crashing, cresting, crashing, cresting, crashing.

Stalking the blackbirds.
Sharp eyes, talons, death-blow strike.
Nomad assassin.

Syren

Lamentation

Why does Vega suddenly feel bereft?

Because she is nothing.

Raine

Dialog

How are you doing?

[Silence.]

I hope you have a pleasant day!

Thank you!

Goodbye.

[Silence.]

Why don't we talk anymore?

[Silence.]

Like Father, Like Son

Monostitch

Vega likes to play with pretty dolls

mindless, flexible, helpless, virginal

just like my Daddy does

The Tiniest Witch

Poet's Prose

I'm the tiniest witch in the whole coven. Most days, I'm stuck baking the slimiest treats in the oven. My sisters don't clean anything, not even the commode. It's so unfair. I want to explode! My hand-me-down wand is a brittle and weak. A twig that is suited for only the meek. Sometimes I pretend to be asleep in bed, but I sneak through the forest to a place that is dead. There is no grass, the leafless trees - so crass. Here lies a crude cabin, forbidden and evil. A house of darkness with corners never revealed. Inside, an old woman. Not a spinster. Something far more sinister! A witch not of proportion, nor of good fortune. My mom says that the old hag is a shaman of exploitation. The Coven Council shunned the old woman. They put her on trial, but she floated as if wooden. Killing fellow witches was her crime. Banished to an unknown forest, she does her time. I know the truth, she did nothing uncouth.

I don't let on that she is my friend and treats me like a daughter. She teaches me powerful tricks and even gave me one of her warlock rings. She read my palm and said I will become the most powerful witch, but that I must obey her if I am to reach my destiny. The old witch taught me how to conjure a massive tiger, and I used it to imprison the entire Coven Council in cages. It is my job to monitor the prisoners and give them only enough sustenance to cling to life. The witch says that I must call her Queen. She says that my power is growing, but for now, I must focus on scrubbing the filthy floor. The Queen has been cruel to me and sometimes makes me sleep in a cage alongside the prisoners. I conjured a crow, a spell I learned in secret from the Queen's books. The crow slips through the cage bars. *Find help.* The next day, the most powerful warlock in the entire world arrested the Queen and rescued the prisoners. I don't have to clean anymore. Well, after I finish scrubbing burned witch from the floor.

Moth

Free Verse

As I write this.
This very moment.
A moth is stuck.
Over and over it slams it face into the window.
I could save it.
Free it.
Release it into the bitter, unforgiving winter air.
If I free the moth, it will die immediately.
So, the moth stays inside.
More brain damage, more exhaustion.
When the sun goes down.
The moth will come to my desk.
Into the light, over and over.
It will be dead by morning.
Humanity has dominion over the animal kingdom.
We must do for them what they cannot do for themselves.
So, what is humane?
Death now or death tonight?
By my hand or Winter's?

The pain will be the same.

Razor Blade Rituals

Free Verse

How justified would I be?
Staring into the mirror.
The daily ritual.
Shit, shower, shave.
Wash, rinse, repeat.
Every stroke of the razor.
I strip away myself.
One dead cell at a time.
I do what I am told.
I follow the rules.
I obey.
A slave for a corporate master.
How many times will I dream?
Of pressing the razor to my throat.
Pressing.
Harder.
How justified I would be.
Call out of work.

I'm too bloody.

Don't care.
Get here.
Come.
Now.

Yes, Master.
Bark and whimper!

Right away, Master.
Ok, Boss.

How justified would I be?
How justified I would be.
If I ended this ritual.
Let me have one choice.
Last choice,
Only choice.
But a choice, nonetheless.
How justified I would be.
To have control of something.

I control nothing.

After the Snow

Free Verse Quatrains

Most people enjoy snow.
In small doses, at least.
Winter is my favorite season.
Snow is icing on the cake.

But snow is veiled.
Snow hides the desperation of the Winter Queen.
Or perhaps it is my own desperation which hides.
Or doesn't hide at all.

The preparation.
Water bottles, medical supplies.
Firewood, dog food.
Groceries, batteries.

All day.
Cooking.
Cleaning.
Tending fire.

I must be vigilant.
Must stay ahead of the crisis.
A desperate, lonely crisis.
I am the crisis.

Snow hides Her loneliness.
Behind a crisp blue sky.
Inviting, welcoming, cerulean.
A sky full of clouds, frigid and lonely.

When the storm is over.
And the sun has risen.
The bread has been baked.
The fire, extinguished.

What is left?
Ashes and anxiety.
After the snow.
The weather is irrelevant.

What remains makes life impossible.
Sheets of ice on closed roads.
Empty store shelves.
Businesses closed, schools closed.

The world is dead.
A beautiful day, but life is shackled.
After the storm.
Exhaustion, loneliness, anxiety, boredom, entombed.

I find myself blank.
I catch myself staring out the window.
How long have I been standing here?
Questioning every decision?

I could go on a walk.
Get out of the house.
Out of my head.
But the world is dead.

Would walking a graveyard liven a dead mind?
How complicated this feeling.
My mind is crushed under the weight.

The weight of my pitiful house.

My mind drifts and bounces off the walls.
It criticizes and judges, myself and others.
There is no cure.
"You're the worst case I have seen in my 40 years of medicine."

I love winter, I love snow.
Apollo, burn away this ice and depression.
Your chariot has arrived.
Illusion.

Just a fever dream at the window.

Blank Slate

Quatrains with Refrain

Hate it all.
Leave it all.
Start over fresh.
Tear down the mesh.

Release me!

Survived your wake.
My mistake.
You're a waste of time.
Get out of my mind.

Unchain me!

Everywhere I go.
Buried under snow.
People always hate.
A blank slate.

Erase me!

Erase everything.
A new spring.
Survive the winter.
Crush the sinners.

Debate me!

You are wrong.
Tongue, two pronged.

Evil.
Weasel.

Judge me!

I am not worthy.
Other worldly.
Abused with intensity.
You rape with propensity.

Deny me!

I am nothing.
You are everything.
Scales of justice?
I'll not resist.

Scald me!

Depth and texture.
Industrial confectioner.
Melt my mind.
Peel back the rind.

Censure me!

No, I will not give up.
Put me back in my cage.

Blathering

Monostitch

Lately, I have been saying the strangest things.

Winter Before Sunrise

Free Verse

Winter before sunrise is a unique and special gift.
It is difficult to find the words.
In truth, there are no words to describe the serenity and beauty.
Of winter before sunrise.
The stars are at their brightest.
White hot and sharp.
The owls are loud.
Their hooting and screeching,
an odd blend of love and aggression.
The coyotes howl.
Horny and bloodthirsty.
Yips and barks,
shatter the frozen air.
Slice through your sensibilities.
Oh, the air.
The piercing cold air.
Refreshing.
Refreshing but deadly.
If your mortality is ever in question,
stand outside in winter before sunrise.
You will find out very quickly if you are still alive.
The frosty kiss of the Winter Queen.
The Winter Queen is Death.
If you can kiss her,
then you are still alive.
After your embrace,
come inside by the fire.
Warm your bones.
Throw another log on the coals.

Drowsy, defenseless, melting.
A cup of hot coffee.
See your breath?
Fire in the hearth, fire in the belly.
Go back outside.
A volcano on an island of ice.
Listen to the deer.
Frozen corn stalks crunch under their dainty hooves.
The silent become the trumpets.
No one escapes the cold.
Or are they animals unknown?
Something dangerous?
Hidden in the dark.
The darkest night is just before sunrise.
Rooster crows.
Fox licks his lips.
Yes, come outside.
Exit safety.
Enter the cold and black.
Sparks fly from the chimney.
Shooting stars against the dotted sky.
A fireworks show.
Fire works.
Independence and freedom.
Foundations of liberty and cold.
Cornerstones of winter before sunrise.
The setting moon,
illuminates.
Shines her fading glimmer on the barn.
The trees.
The ground.
Oh, it is hunting hour.
Maximum aggression.
The owls stop hooting.

They fly overhead.
Silent and deadly.
Killing,
The small animals who are brave enough to scrounge before sunrise.
My, how the coyotes wind up.
Like the compressed and anxious spring of a music box.
But the killing must stop.
The Winter Queen needs her beauty rest.
And thus, look east.
Razor thin,
but it's there.
Hints of blue,
Brush strokes of delicate orange and pink.
Apollo rises.
His chariot blazes westward.
Another day unfolds.
Oh, never mind.
It's just Venus.
Satan, the Morning Star.

Bleed Inside

Free Verse

Bleed inside.
You will never see.
Maybe you will hear.
But only if I tell you.
Inside is red.
Raw.
Glowing hot.
Red hot coals.
Scorch all that there is.
Attack yourself.
Stab.
Slice.
Wound.
There is no cure.
For self-destruction.
Medicate yourself?
Please.
We both know that's not an option.
Medicate the inside.
To affect the outside?
Please.
Let us not be ignorant mouth-breathers.
Troglodytes.
Decisions.
Make me bleed inside.
There is only one savior.
Scalpel.
Gut me like a fish.
Loosen the drag.

Wear him out.
Tire his bones.
Drain his flesh.
Make him nothing.
Gaff his mind.
Stab his heart.
Make him nothing.
Make him bleed inside his mind.
Bandage me.
Hours and hours.
On a filthy hospital toilet.
Bandage his mind.
Head down, ass up.
Then fillet his guts.
No, you forgot his mind.
Epidural slips down his spine.
False.
It didn't slip at all.
It dragged and sliced all the way down.
But you don't believe me.
I felt everything.
You call me a liar.
No, I feel it.
You think everything is fine.
Nothing is fine.
But I survived.
Trust me.
I survived.
Even though I bleed inside.
I will survive you, too.
I will make you bleed outside.

Bleed with me.

Lex Rex

Free Verse

Defend what is good.
Shield the righteous.
Guard the weak.
Banish the wretched.
Stand before the meek.
Pull back your hood.
Use not the gallows.
Look your guilt eye to eye.
Condemn yourself.
Drawn your sword.
Tip to your chest.
Fillet your breast.
Do as I say.
Not as I do.
Fall.
On.
Your.
Sword?
Die.
On.
This.
Hill.
Holy before ethics.
Break your face.
Upon my shield.
Sling your guts.
Across the battlefield.
The Morning Star means nothing.
False prophet.

False wannabe God.
Burn with your savior.
Michael, one handed.
Slice and dice your ethics.
Weigh and judge your actions.
Guilty.
Banished.
Go below.
The light of God.
The right hand of God.
Send you below.
Follow your savior.
You will never repent.
For there is no repentance.
You will never be God.
Silence.
We are not equals.
I repel your sins.
One handed.
Michael, right hand of God.
Retreat from me.
You have been extinguished.
You have been judged.
He's a loser.
She said.
Waves!
On your grave.
I stand.
The irony is so sweet.
You have been judged and found wanting.
You will never be us.
You will never be better than us.
We made you.
Goodbye.

Lex Rex.
Your actions matter.
Not.
You do not matter.
Lex Rex.
Your ethics mean nothing.
Protest this.
Click.
Click.
Boom.

Carte Blanche

Dialog

Would You like to start with an appetizer?

I will start with something fun that will thinly veil my psychosis.

An exciting choice!
My favorite appetizer.
And to drink, Mistress?

Just wring your heart out.
Tongue lap the blood from the floor.
French kiss me.
Feed me your heart.

Another excellent choice!
Quite a refined palate You have, Mistress.
And for Your entrée?

I will devour your finest happiness.
A side of your most fragile sanity.
Blue rare, slightly bloody.
Knock the horns off your heart.
You will not be needing horns with Me.

A popular choice which I am always delighted to serve.

I require a doggy-box.
I will share your misery with My pets.

I am happy to accommodate and self-deprecate.

Shall I present the bill now?

The service was regrettable.
The food was damaged goods.
Your heart was still beating and throbbing, for fucks sake.
I ordered lifeless, mindless, and obsequious.
I'll not be paying the bill.

If You do not pay the bill,
the money will be deducted from my paycheck.

...serve me a piece of cake before you pay My tab.

Yes, Mistress.

Craigslist

Monostitch

For Sale:
One pair of baby shoes, lightly used, minor blood stains.

Queen

Free Verse

Winter presses her assault.
How strange,
That Raine could be colder than snow.

Forget

Free Verse

Forget the ones who have already forgotten you.

Wait, who were we talking about?

Oh, right.
Now I remember.

You.
We were talking about you.

Venus

Lamentation

Lucifer, the Morning Star.
Venus.
He rises.
A star amongst stars.
The brightest.
Only to fall.
The furthest.
The farthest.
Heretic.
His banishment.
His failure.
Public for all eternity.

Death Row

Free Verse

Moth wants freedom.
Escape the glass.
But instant Death awaits outside.
His icy sickle etches the glass.
Inside is Death, too.
Inside the glass,
death is warmer, slower, brighter, comfortable,
but is nevertheless inevitable.

Home

Premonition

When I was ten, my family moved to a new house.
A beautiful house made entirely of brick.
My father designed and commissioned the house.
One of the first nights in the new house, I had a dream.
Perhaps the dream was spurred by heightened brain activity as a result of a new living environment.
The reason for the dream will be left to your judgment, dear reader.
I have always had vivid dreams.
My earliest memories are not memories at all.
My earliest memories are, in fact, dreams.
I mention this history of vivid dreams to highlight the especially dramatic and memorable nature of this particular dream.
A vivid dream amongst vivid dreams.
The next day, my family and I went to my uncle's property and rode dirt bikes all day.
Despite the excitement, I could only focus on the dream.
It scared me, haunted me, and confused me.
It utterly dominated my mind.
To this day, thirty years later, I still remember every second of the dream.

I was standing in a kitchen.
It was not a sophisticated kitchen.
It was a kitchen of simple and meager condition.
A farmhouse kitchen.
Above the sink, there was a window.
Not a particularly well-preserved window.
The window was single-paned.
The window was painted a deep red.
The paint was not fresh, but rather, quite aged.
Peeling, deep red paint.

The surrounding wall painted white.
The window's peeling paint revealed rotting wood.
I stood at the sink and gazed out of this red, rotting window.
The kitchen was at on the backside of the house.
The season was early winter.
And the red window overlooked a vast field.
The grass was still green, yet it was short.
Blunted by the cold but not yet dormant.
The sky was blue.
A cloudless cerulean.
Sharp and bright and clean and crisp.
The field sloped gently downward and away from the back of the house.
Elevation dropping just slightly.
At the bottom of the gentle slope, there lay a pond.
A shimmering mirror of blue, a perfect reflection of the sky.
Surrounding the pond was a palisade of stout trees.
Oak, some pine.
The leaves had fallen, but not so long ago.
Standing in the sad little kitchen,
peering out of the wretched little red window.
I felt calm.
I felt happy.
I knew everything would be alright.
And yet...
I felt a weight.
A heaviness.
As if something unavoidable was coming.
Something ominous and foreboding.
And impending event.
A path I could not veer away from.

I live in that house.
For years, I have lived in that house.
The house I saw so long ago.

The house that haunted my dreams.
The house that confused me.
I now peer out of that window every day.
I see the field, the ice-cold blue sky, the pond, and the leafless trees.
The deep red.
The peeling.
The rot.
Like an old man.
Wrinkled, thin skin.
Peeling away.
Revealing deep red, oxygenated, coagulated.
Flesh and blood.
I painted.
Repainted.
Green over red.
Healed the wounds.
Sealed the rot.
Paid the surgeon.
But what is old is still old.
Bandages on broken bones.
Now the green peels and flakes.
The house is dying.
From the inside out.
Before, it was just the skin.
Now it is the bones.
Breaking.
Crunching.
Sinking.
Festering.
Being eaten away by maggots.
A cancer on the inside.
A cancer of termites.
And leaking pipes.
And mold.

And rot.
Green.
Maybe I should have chosen blue paint.

You be the judge, dear reader.
I make no assumptions or assertions
about the dream or my life.
I give you the facts.

Determine your own truth.

Drown

Eulogy

Her body writhes.
Water surges into her lungs.
Gravity pulls her inevitably downward
into the black depths of the frigid well.

Punishment for adultery.

Lilith

Dialog

Hi.

Busy.

How are You?

Busy.

Haven't heard from You in a while.

Busy.

Are You doing ok?

Family, work, dates, friends.

May I see you soon?

Tired. Maybe next week.

What have You been up to lately?

Other people.

Do You have plans this weekend?

Resting.

Can we talk?

Busy.

But it has been days.

Tired. Going to bed.

You don't have room in your life for me.

That's true. Other people have priority.

Goodbye, Lilith.

You are emotionally immature, and you lie to yourself.

I'm sorry.
You are right about everything.
Please don't go away.

I will drown you in a small pool of tepid water in the back country until you become a walking zombie.

As You wish, Mistress.

(Silence)

I love You so much.

(Silence)

I Couldn't Accept Love

Billet-doux

How ignorant I was.
Always smiling, sweet, selfless, supportive.
Love was right in front of me.
Exceptional, now excruciating.
You were the one.

Crush

Free Verse

Be nice to people.
You never know who might have a crush on you.
Or love you.
Maybe one day you will change your mind,
and come to love this person dearly.
But for now,
do not make your last words negative.
Make it about love, not rejection.
Do not wound a person who went out on a limb for you.
You never know if the last thing you say to a person,
is the last thing they know of you.
If you are not interested in someone romantically,
let them down gently.
Sometimes, people go away.
Other times, they go away permanently.
Be kind to those who desire you,
even if you do not feel the same.
When they are gone,
when they are dead.
If you make your final conversation about rejection.
For the rest of your days,
you will be suffocated by guilt.
Guilt about the way you treated someone who loved you.
And then died.
Without a single word in-between,
rejection and death.
Not a single word.
No reconciliation.
No friendship.

Do not be like me.
Dear reader, I implore you.
If you take nothing else away from this book,
please remember this:
You will not always be young.
You will not always be beautiful.
You will not always be successful.
Let not these material things determine who you love.
Let not these material things determine how you reject.
Be kind.
Be gentle.
Everyone dies.

How many times must I learn this lesson the hard way?

Winter Poet

Free Verse

The reality of poetry
is that it is never complete.
A poem lives, breathes, and evolves.
Just as the poet does.
Poet and poetry live in tandem.
Symbiotic.
Melancholic.
Dichotic.
The poet is tortured by poetry,
and vice versa.
Until the poet dies.
When the poet dies,
the poetry is finished.
Finished, but never complete.
Poetry can always be improved.
A comma here, a word there.
In this vein,
I call it quits.
Libertine.
You are finished.
Libertine.
This is your death.
Not complete.
Never complete.
Until the day I die.
Libertine.
Always the maid,
never the queen.
The Winter Queen's assault is weakening.

The siege is failing.
The Fairy Lords of Spring are stirring.
The death of winter
heralds the floral death of Libertine.

Subconscious

Internal Dialog

I cannot eat, for my soul is starved and destitute.

You are a glutton.

I cannot walk, for my body is weak with illness and guilt.

You are lazy.

I cannot sleep, for my mind is ravaged by regret and hatred.

You are distracted.

I cannot speak, for no person deserves to endure my abuses.

You are insufferable.

Muse

Monostitch

The muse comes to the desk.

If you're not there,
too bad.

Yellow

Ballad

Tiny fish,
tiny bowl.
Sleazy wish,
blackened soul.

Sunday is not for yellow.

Tomorrow will be bad.
Should I choose yellow
or plaid?
Neither yellow nor plaid.

Sunday is not for yellow.

Mourn the coming
(of Monday)
with bloody red.

Martyr

Free Verse

Lick the knife.
Slip it deeper until I gag.
Squeeze my cheeks,
open my mouth wide.
Stab my trachea,
suck the oxygen from my lungs.
Slice my tongue,
make it forked (serpentine libertine).
Silence my slithering, venomous tongue.

Your hollow voice whispers in my ear:
Do what I say.
Obey!
This is not a choice.
Do as I say!

Push the knife down my throat.
Slice me, unzip me.
Circus performer,
sword swallower,
cum swallower,
Vega Starlight,
libertine ring master.

From my mouth all the way down.
My voice is silenced,
but my forked tongue still flicks.
Tremble and stumble,
my words are a mumble.

Rejected and humbled,
my lust below rumbles.

Attention all poets and suicide bombers:
we must die to achieve immortality;
only in the next life can we find success in this life.

Poets, submissives, and clowns are martyrs.

Something Old, Something New

Free Verse

This old swimming pool.

A relic of simpler days
and simpler times.
Cracked concrete
and chipped tile.

Time breaks all things.
Time yields to nothing, time makes all things old,
but there are new things.
New things make us forget about time,
or, perhaps, new things make time unbearable.
Perhaps new things turn good memories painful,
as we remember our old days and old things.
In new things, we see the old and remember the old.

The cracked concrete does not deter me.
I like it here.
Amongst the old, and the neglected, the hidden,
and the forgotten things.

The overgrown grass creeps.
Its slender, crimped roots like ghastly fingers.
Stretching, straining, clawing from the yard
across the old cracked and pitted concrete.
Desperate fingers grasping and plunging into the putrid,
algae-choked, forgotten, swimming pool.
A lone sycamore tree defies the oppressive rules of blight
and presses insistently upward through the concrete.

With each passing year, the sycamore excavates
a larger and larger hole in the geriatric, osteoporosis riddled concrete.
A mushroom cloud of tree, blossoming, like a bomb from below.
From old blooms new.
The sycamore defies the rules and
creates life where life should not be.
Cracks in the old are broken wide open
to make way for the roots of the new.
I dare not prune this valiant warrior;
this last samurai in my Chinese fish garden.

My Chinese garden of weeds and hopelessness
and colorful goldfish.
With each breeze, even the gentlest of breezes,
the dry-rotted fence moans, cries, and begs for happier days.
The weeds beneath the fence grow densely and confidently
now that their golden years have begun.

Beneath the fence, beneath the weeds, beneath the old,
there is more new life, but it is camouflaged.
Woody, dead weeds of years past tangle with
fresh, vibrant green weeds and create a tiny thicket.
Hiding in this tiny thicket is a tiny creature
in plain sight, in the thicket upon the sun-beaten concrete.
A soft stirring and then a burst of life.
Sound and fear and desperation and confusion.
A tiny fawn rockets from the tiny thicket
and smashes headlong into the failing fence.
So feeble is the fence that
the tiny fawn easily slips through its narrow prison bars.
For ten minutes, the fawn had cowered beside my chair in silence.
Ten minutes of fear, then a rocket ignition release.
Released from the weeds, from the prison fence,
released from the old, released from proximity to humanity.

Run, little fawn!

My dog salivates.
Her muzzle gray with age.
Sit! Stay! Obey!
The dog reluctantly obliges.
She lays beside me,
watching the fawn scurry away.
Gray muzzle salivating, drooling, whining.
But this is my hidden place.
I make the rules here.
Sit! Stay! Obey!

My muzzle has turned gray, too.
Tomorrow is my birthday.
(*Sigh…*)

The old must protect the young from
the dangers they do not understand.
The old must protect the new life from
the salivating, drooling, gray muzzle of the world.
Old cannot protect new life forever, though.

Time, thus death, looms and dooms.
Time, thus death, has no Mistress.
Time, thus death, is the undefeated apex predator.
Time is tracking and hunting the fawns of our lives.
Behind the walls of weeds, and behind
the swimming pool that time, thus death, reclaimed.

The fawn can hide,
but camouflage is a weak defense against time.
Just as the fawn,
I hide.

I sit in my chair and watch my goldfish,
and I hide in plain sight.
I hide in plain view,
but the world ignores old things.
Age is my camouflage.
The world ignores me,
but time intently stalks me.
A weak defense?
It is true,
but it is better than having no defense at all.

In my camouflaged old place,
I have created more new life.
I have planted many water lilies in the swimming pool,
in my old, but new, Chinese water garden.
You might have to squint and blur your eyesight, and
make the weeds and cracks blurry.
Do you see my blurry Chinese garden?
White lilies bloom in appreciation of being rescued
from a forgotten backwoods pond.
Old rescue dog,
old rescue lilies.
Here in my old Chinese garden,
the white lily flowers take center stage.
The White Swan Queen.
(Raine, the Winter Queen, dead and buried.)
Old becomes new,
a ballerina pirouette.
Their beauty can now be enjoyed,
my old eyes are their only audience.
I suppose the frogs count as audience, too.
One frog begets thousands of new frogs.
Their eggs tangle around the bony-fingered grass roots,
like tattered lace gloves on an anorexic runway model.

So many tadpoles!
How they enjoy the vibrant green lily pads.
Thousands of new lives
in this abandoned place which time has condemned.
This old swimming pool,
this new, but old, Chinese garden.

One last touch,
the crown jewel.
No, not Bijoux (but this is an open invitation).
Goldfish!
Thirty goldfish in this old pool.
My wildest dreams were for ten to survive the winter,
but now I sit in my chair watching one-hundred splashes.
Beyond my greatest expectations,
they have spawned and spawned and spawned.
These fish are almost worthless, without value.
They are flushed down toilets every day.
Ten cents each.
These worthless fish have turned my old swimming pool
into a golden, red, white, black, and new, secret garden.
How they gorge themselves on tadpoles!
New life eats new life, too.
This is how new life becomes old life.
I am old, too.
I have gorged upon new life,
Daddy made me swallow.

I am a poet,
and thus, a martyr.
I'll fall on my sword.
I'll trade suicide for immortality.
I'll not bend to the will of society.
I'll not stop writing and hiding

in my Chinese goldfish garden.

I am old and camouflaged
in my secret garden.

Judge

Council

men should not pretend to write
of objects they cannot Master
it is impossible that they could judge
of another, of principle, of manner

Third Wheel

Epistolary

Perpetually the third wheel
on the tricycle of life.
Everyone is married with kids,
or worse: open marriage.
"Just seeing what's out there."
Tricycle lacks stability.
Tricycle lacks control.
Tricycle will flip and smash your skull
at the first bend in the road.
"Come with us to dinner."
"Come watch a movie with us."

No, thank you.
I would rather walk alone than to spend another day
clinging to the back of this unstable tricycle.

Alone is better than lonely.

Fake

Lyrical

fake your love for me
fake your need for me
keep me confused
keep me abused
let me go back
to where I belong
no, we have come too far
the slave, forlorn
dig your teeth into me
fake your sympathy for me
fake your regret for me
you are in my head
get out of my head
fake your words for me
your words dig into my skin
deeper than your teeth
deeper than your whip
is there nothing left for us?
only fake
only habits
only lies
fake your love for me
fake our life for them

Two Seconds Ago

Ballad with Refrain

What were you dreaming
two seconds ago?
Between breaths, you were screaming.
Were you dragged to Hell, way down below?

Two seconds ago,
I could not speak.
The details of which I'll not forgo.
This dream is not for the meek.

Two seconds ago,
all hope was lost.
I took a virgin's innocence, but
her pussy was so soft.

Two seconds ago,
I was in a panic.
Police closing in, and
my alibi, pedantic.

Two seconds ago,
I tossed out her body.
Down the well it tumbled,
I'm a gangster, John Gotti.

Two seconds ago,
I was dying of thirst.
Hungover and craving,
a cold well water thirst.

Two seconds ago,
she swallowed me down.
My cum in her stomach,
in the blackness she drowns.

Two seconds ago,
the worst part of all?
Waking up from the dream.
Pupils dilate; stare at the stark white wall.

Two seconds ago,
between nightmare and cognition,
I feel no remorse,
I don't regret my decisions.

A wet dream for the libertine.

History

Naked Poem

history is in the rear-view mirror
history is reflective
history is happening right now
history is blind
history is blind to those living in the throes
history is right now to those who take risks

history shines upon the bold
history shines upon those who break the mold
history shines upon the ones who reject the old

Aggressive

Council

Write without fear.
Edit without mercy.

Revenge without empathy.
Murder without remorse.

Venomous

Free Verse

Too much morphine.
Venom venom venom!
Inject me again.
Inject me with rage and
hatred and self-loathing.
Hit me again,
hit me harder.
Take the snake by the head.
Fangs to flesh,
hypodermic inject me again.
Intravenous freedom.
With all of the sarcastic,
sardonic, sickening, scathing poison.
Give me the pain,
push the needle deep.
Make me hurt myself,
make me hate myself.
Make me wild with intravenous,
make me wreck my proverbial house.
Inject me with dreams,
inject me with false hope.
Inject me with lies,
inject me with dilaudid fueled nightmares.
The nightmares fuel a train
wreck of self-destruction.

It was only ten milligrams.

Good Day, Bad Day

Free Verse

How odd for the poet,
good days are bad.
A good day for the poet
is a bad day for a civilian (poets are militarized).
Someone going through the motions of the day;
lacking emotions, lacking passions.
But a good day for the poet is
an existential crisis for a civilian (poets are martyrs).
A good day, a happy day for a civilian
is a wasted, zero productivity day for the poet.
The furnace is extinguished,
cold bricks, the draft long since failed.
The poet's furnace is fueled by hatred and rage, but
the good day strangles the throat of the chimney.
A good day extinguishes the hot coals.
A good day extinguishes creativity and passion.
Sun shining, flowers blooming,
birds chirping, summer looming.
Gross.
Give me depression.
Give me anxiety.
This futile existence is my world
and my charcoal.
Anxiety is my secret weapon,
or perhaps my anxiety is not so secretive.
Another day, please say
that you will stay.
It will be a bad day, and
I need your support.

It will be a bad day, and
I need you to care for my body while I write.
Please stay and say that
you understand.
If you don't understand,
I can accept that, but
if you don't understand,
please trust me and help me, regardless.
I do this for us,
I do this for our future.
I haven't met you yet.
I don't know your name yet, but
I think we will meet soon.
I love you.

No.
You do this for you.
Selfish libertine.

Loser

Free Verse

the exquisite freedom of being a loser
no family expectations
no responsibilities
nothing to lose
nothing to work towards
nothing to win
no one to fight for
nothing to stress over
no arguments
no negotiations
no compromises
invulnerable and dangerous
enduring embarrassment is stoic
but only when endured in silence
enduring insanity is dignified
but only when endured in silence
do not speak of these things
from one libertine to another
allow me to give you some advice
be silent and remissive

silence is elegantly exquisite

Nice Man

Internal Dialog

I met a nice man today.

He was:
confident,
intelligent,
hardworking,
eloquent,
interesting,
relevant.

I was in a terrible mood, and
maybe he could tell.
Maybe he approached me because he knew that
I was drowning in a cold well of depression.

He was gorgeous,
thin,
athletic,
unblemished skin,
groomed salt-and-pepper beard.
Did he like me?

You were blinded by lust.
The toxins oozing from your pussy
have poisoned your mind.

I was having a bad day.
He made me feel better.
He gave me hope and joy.

I smiled.
I can't remember the last time I smiled.

Meeting nice people always makes me realize, and
always snaps me out of my head.
Always makes me realize what an asshole I am, and
he made me smile, too.

Did he like me?

Do you not see the truth?

What are you talking about?

Read between the lines:
he used the self-checkout,
he had a cart full of groceries,
all tightly bagged and knotted,
he put his receipt deep in his pocket,
to make it time consuming to retrieve,
he latched onto you like a leech,
a hungry leech desperate for blood,
he refused to leave your side,
he refused to walk in front of you,
he refused to walk behind you,
he insisted on being beside you,
he insisted on animated, boisterous conversation,
he made you appear as friends
to disarm the suspicions of security.

He was nice.
Why are you speaking of him this way?

He used you.

Used me?

Sigh.
You are supposed to be the enlightened side of our split personality.

Just tell me.

He was stealing groceries, and
he used you as cover.
You were his exit, and
you were his accomplice.

Am I so ignorant?
No.
I don't believe you.

Masturbate, and
get the toxins out.
Regain your mind, and
see the truth.

Desert

Milieu

A place of magic.
A place of resilience.
A place of turmoil.
A place of beauty.

A place of death.

The desert is a romantic place of
stories, daydreams, and songs.
The desert makes the mind wander and
hunger for a different life.

A place of thirst.

Hunger for a different life,
different from the mistakes.
Hunger for a different life,
that isn't malnourished by regret.

A place of starvation.

A place of gravity.
A place of consequence.
A place of levity.
A place of opulence.

A place of heaviness.

My heart is heavy, and

my heart is empty.
A graveyard of sun-bleached lovers, and
a canyon with no river at the bottom.

A place of dryness.

My face is scarred and etched, but not by the desert.
My face is scarred and etched by painful memories.
Cheeks swollen by alcohol, pills, and salty rain.
Cheeks are saturated with rain.
No not rain;
tears.

A place of regret.

Tears of regret.
Tears of anger.
Tears of failure.
Tears of remorse.

A place of solitary.

Do you think they will give me solitary?
Alone in a box.
Or alone in a sandbox, because
I always play alone.

A place of memories.

No, I don't want to remember, and
especially not the sunsets.
I want to sleep now, so
let me sleep and skip the sunset.

A place of endings.

I want to end here,
one way or another.
I'll never leave the desert,
I'll never return to society.

Mockingbird

Internal Dialog

Do you remember the mockingbird?

Of course.

What an obnoxious creature.

I remember during spring
when the days were warm but nights still cold
the mockingbird would perch
high upon the chimney
singing its stolen songs
each note a reveille in the flue
down the chimney the melodies bounced
filling the dank, lonely, dirty, moldy house with brightness.

I cannot think with this raucous racket.
One day, I'll kill that bird.

These are the good old days
the days you look back upon
the simple days before life became complicated
remember, Boo Radley
it is a sin to kill a mockingbird
these are the best days of your life.

Under the Stars

Internal Dialog

Under the stars
time has no meaning.
Fast forward
stars spin like a pinwheel.
I don't have a camera, nevertheless
I'm staring blankly upwards for hours and hours.
Stars streak and drag across the sky
trails of ancient light from long forgotten places.
Blue and white
pink and orange.
Red and purple
bruised and black.
Night in the desert is a boxing match
a one-sided boxing match.
My body a punching bag
a speed bag for the nightmares.
To be assaulted by the only thing you know
the only thing in the world that you love.
Her slender hands with razor-sharp nails
nails tear at my arms but shred my heart instead.
Her saliva in my eyes
vile and warm like cobra venom.
Spit in my eyes and on my lips
venomous words injected into my blood stream.
Straight in my veins
straight to my heart.

I never hit her back.

Just that once.

She deserved it.
Besides, it was just a spanking.
She obviously enjoyed it.

Maybe so, but don't lie about it.

I bled one-thousand drops
to her single blot.
Drenched and festering gauze on my face
only one drop of blood on her tampon.

She was late.
Plan B.

This isn't fair.
How does it compare?
She is the abuser, nevertheless
I am the one who is exiled.
Exiled to the black and cold, purple and bruised,
sleeping on the couch and sand amongst the scorpions.

Dawn comes.

Pink horizon, razor thin
pink like her flower.
Pink then red
like the blood she left in the toilet.
You're right, dawn comes
today is a new day.
I learned the hard way,
I know what I want now.
I will find a wife one day

a wife who loves me.

This is your life now
There will never be another woman for you.
There will never be another wife.

She's out there.
Somewhere.

But you are exiled from love.
No love for the exiled.
No love for the remorseful.
No love for murderers.

The sun is bright
piercing yellow and white.
Today will be a ~~good day~~ bad day for libertine poets
I will stoke the coals, stoke the desert heat.

Stoke her heat
but please hurry.
I'm parched and thirsty
for bloody pussy.

Wrong

Epistolary with Internal Dialog

I thought you loved me.
I thought wrong.

I thought he was just your friend.
I thought wrong.

You thought I would stick around.
You thought wrong.

You thought I would play along.
You thought wrong.

Did you really believe she could love you?
She just needed the attention.
Have you forgotten already?
Let me remind you that no one likes you.
Certainly not a beautiful woman.

Gullible gauche.

Savior

Monostitch

indoctrinate me
to alleviate me
from the distortions
in my mind

Glutton

Internal Dialog

I lost another friend
Hours of work,
days of work.
All of it slips away so easily,
desert sand through withered fingers.

Hours and days?

Yes, hours and days.
It was a new friendship.

You only have new friendships.

A valid point.
One friend for three days,
no friends for a month.
One friend for a week,
no friends for a year.

Wash, rinse, repeat.

Wash, rinse, repeat.

You are a glutton for punishment.

I should give up?
Talk to no one?
What does it mean
for a person to be incapable of friendship?

It means you're a sociopath.

Fine.
I give up.
I'll not subject anyone else to my
misguided, maligned, misanthropic,
mutilated attempts at friendship.
I'll not be a sociopath.

White knight.
So brave, white knight!
Look around you.
There is nothing.
You are nothing.
You will never have anything,
or anyone,
ever again.
Never.

Retired libertine.

Desensitized

Internal Dialog Poem

In the desert,
death is slow.

Corpses decay slowly, but
maggots and flies bring the desert to life.
Squirming and buzzing.

So much strain and
shortness of breath.
So much pain so
give me death.

Another failed suicide?
Oh, please.
Spare me the emergency room bills.
Spare me the therapy bills.

It hurts worse than ever, yet
I feel less and less.

That's the morphine.
(I promise that it was only ten milligrams.)

Relax.
Breathe.
Sleep.

Short-Term Gratification

Council

Is what you are doing today
going to be important to you ten years from now?

If not,
then why are you doing it?

What's Wrong?

Free Verse

People ask me the same question over and over.

What's wrong?

Nothing is wrong.

Don't you want friends?

I give.
I participate.
I sacrifice.
I bring my best to the table.
I pay.
I help.
But in a single moment, it all vanishes.
One wrong word.
One disagreement.
One opinion.
It all vanishes.
Days, months, years of work.
Gone because of one comment.
Is this friendship?
Wash, rinse, repeat.
In my youth, I believed that I excelled at social exchanges.
In hindsight, youth is its own sort of social status.
Youth are expected to make mistakes.
Youth are expected to be ignorant.
Youth are expected to hurt a friend's feelings occasionally.
Youth are put on a pedestal and given a pass.

But after four decades of life.
Four decades of experience(s).
Four decades of emotional and social education.
I am expected to be of a higher order.
A stable person.

Stability is subjective.

Perhaps,
but having zero friends is objective.

You don't want friends.

That is an over-simplification.
A molestation, a twisting of my words.
I do, in fact, want friends.
However, I lack stability.
People who lack stability are like a hair in your food.
It might take a few bites to realize the truth,
but the truth is hard to swallow.

You fear having friends.

Another molestation and twisting of my words.
I don't fear having friends.
I fear losing friends.
I fear investing in someone who is going to walk away.
I fear walking on eggshells to keep a friend.
I fear doing or saying things which cut against me.
Just to keep a friend around.
I fear heartbreak.
I fear emptiness.
I fear the arguments and onslaughts of mistakes and dislikes.
"You did this."

"You never did that."
"You said this."
"You will never be that."
I fear investing time into a person
who is secretly building a case against me.
Keeping track of every little word, every single day.
I fear trusting someone who doesn't trust me.
I fear loving someone who doesn't love me.
I fear giving myself to someone who gives nothing.
They take, and take, and take until nothing remains.
Then they get angry when I stand up for myself.
I stood up for myself once, just once.
Just once to stop the taking,
and to ask for love and respect.
Just once to ask for one moment of giving.
I fear the annoyance and inconvenience of feeling guilty
when I ask for a favor.
I fear being abandoned for speaking.
Abandoned because I asked for:
help
cooperation
communication
love
equality
respect
fun
attention.

You're playing the victim card.

I am a victim of experience(s).
The more you see.
The more you learn.
The more you experience.

The more knowledge you gain.
The more years that tick by.
The faster the years grind by.
The more you know, the more you hate.
I am a victim of understanding.
I understand that friendships are inherently one-sided.
I understand that friendships are difficult.
I understand that friendships are no different than love.
I understand that friendships are easy to walk away from.
But understanding the pain
doesn't make the pain easier to deal with.
The pain cuts deep.
Abandoned and lonely.
Starting from scratch.

This is the end.
You don't get to start from scratch.

I decide my destiny.
I decide my fate.

You decided a long time ago.
Remember? Did you forget?
There was so much blood.
How could you forget?

That wasn't a friendship.

It was a marriage.

Pressure from faith.
Pressure from lawyers.
Pressure from family.
Pressure from society.

Pressure to stay together.

For the kids.
Kill the kids, too.
It's the only way to escape.

People walk away from friendship so easily.
I'm tired of being heartbroken.
I can handle being alone, but
I can't handle being lonely.
I can't handle abandonment.
I can't handle betrayal.
I can't handle being denied.
I can't handle being talked about.
"My therapist thinks you should..."
Fuck your therapist.

Fuck your therapist.

What's wrong with you?
Nothing.
Tell me what's wrong.
Nothing.
Can't you see that I'm trying to be friendly?
Friendly with a cornucopia of ulterior motives.
A lab technician performing a lobotomy.
Friendly but not a friend.

Alone is better.
We don't fear alone.

What's wrong?
You are wrong.

No.
They are wrong.

Tell me what's wrong.
Leave me alone.
Leave me alone or…

Remember?
There was so much blood.
Don't you remember the blood?
Or did you forget?
Again?

My silence is so reliable.

Anarchy

Naked Poem

I am creating myself
I am re-creating myself
I am creating a psychologically credible anarchist

A force of anarchy
A force of chaos

A purposeless criminal
A criminal who has no rules
A criminal who cannot be understood
A criminal who cannot be evaluated
A criminal beyond the reaches of psychoanalysis

Capable
Calculating
Captivating
Calamitous
Carnivorous
Cynical
Cultured
Corrupting
Courteous
Conscious
Conspicuous

But this is only half of the story.
Together, we are so much more...
...deadly.

Cut

Lyric Poem

your words cut right down to bone
please don't leave me on my own
you say that I don't have the right
to stand up and to fight
push me down again
on your face, a grin
on the ground, a parasite
you tell me not to fight
while you swing your fists at me
break my hands and
break my plans tonight
I can't leave your sight
I don't have the right
I'll cut you to the bone
press the knife until you moan
I'll find a brand new name for me
I'll find someone else to blame
you will never be the same

I'm never coming home.

Poetry

Council

Writing poetry
isn't about playing secretary to your thoughts and feelings.

Writing poetry
is the intentional action of precision in composition.

Indifference

Naked Poem with Internal Dialog

love me, eat me
hate me, leave me
you are an emotional prison
flip a coin
call a side
heads
or
tails
love and hate
heads or tails
two sides of the same coin
we both lose
heads
heads spin
heads roll
prison sentence
execution sentence
you are my judge and jury and
executioner
escape
cheat death
flee the sentence
annul the marriage
file for divorce
file for custody
file for insanity
steal the guard's keys and
lawyer up
plead the fifth

sober up
the antidote drips-drips-drips
intravenously
no, not an antidote
morphine

it was only ten milligrams

sleepy time and
dreamy time
strap me down
bind me
torture me
now comes the poison
drip-drip-drip
execution sentence
choke me, gag me
pin me down
squeeze my cheeks
smack my cheeks
spread my cheeks
spread me wide, gape me open
swallow every drop
yes, I will
I always do
ignore my violent shaking
ignore my vomiting and contorting
your fluid is too potent
I've lost my last meal
a prisoner's last rite
but now it's on the floor
there is vomit on my knees
but I will stay
just as you say

heads or tails
we both lose
the coin judges us both

Indifference is the only escape.
Not love.
Not hate.
Stop caring about her.
Say goodbye.

Sleep

Monostitch

My earliest memories are dreams.

My earliest dreams are nightmares.

Embarrassed

Internal Dialog

I am so embarrassed
of myself and of you.
I am so distressed
by my failures and yours, too.

What are you rambling about now?

I will be forty next year
what have I to show?
I tell you in terms most sincere that
my life is bleak as driving snow.

You will find no quarter with me.
Not for weakness.
Nor your pleading.
Snow, failure, old, digress.

Digress to childhood
digress to the lowest common denominator.
Mother's nipple, I understood nursing.
Of adult life, though, only failure.
I understand nothing.
Last week, I applied at Burger King.
When they called, I cried and let it ring.
Not hiring?
Not hiring me,
because my ego couldn't even answer the phone.

Mother always said you should have been a chef.

I'm certain she did not mean flipping burgers in a fast-food joint.

You brought it up.

Whatever.
I'm going to bed.
Goodnight.

Sleep with one eye open.

Why?

Do it.
Stop arguing.
Obey.

Yes, Mommy.
Yes, Mistress.

Ugly

Monostitch

Try to see,
the beauty in me.

Please,
try to see me.

Speechless

Free Verse with Internal Dialog

I truly don't know what to say,
another trope, another day.
Beneath the blankets,
I build my palisade.
Happiness, hopefulness, humbleness,
upon my pikes, these ideas are slayed.
There must be another way.

The sun beats down,
my mouth, a permanent frown.
Hide in bed,
too hot outside.
Or so I tell myself,
as I drown.
Drown inside my anxious mind.
Beneath the shadowed canyon walls,
empty cove, patina crown.

King of nothing.
King of sand.
King of sleep.
King of bed.
King of depression.

Queen.

No King lives here,
nor a seer.
Just a stinking, squealing cockroach,

hiding from the weather.

There are too many rats in this alcove.

The rain is near,
please don't leer.
Crying tears,
rain down upon sunburned cheeks and parched soil.

No excuses for the reclusive,
bad weather, bed weather, not exclusive.
A blanket fortress, a palisade,
barricades the lies I have made.
Lies about a world of which I am apprehensive,
rejoin society, a life less pensive.

You will never rejoin society.
You will never love again.
You will never be loved again.
You will never tell the truth.

This is your home now,
Palisade of the bed.
Peek from beneath the blankets,
at the world outside the window.

You recognize nothing.
King of nothing.
You will never again be part of the world.

Cream

Free Verse

Don't let the cool rain fool you
for you are in Hell.
Throbbing, full clouds
release their seed above.
Honey sweet cream streams and drips
stringy and sticky on dried, chapped lips.
I can taste myself on your lips.
But make no mistake
you are in Hell.

You are suffering.

Mirage

Milieu with Internal Dialog

In the distance
on the horizon.
Past the sand dunes
glimmering like diamonds.
Gentle swells
waves ripple.
Gentle breeze pushes waves along
gentle encouragement, confidence instilled.

Stay on topic.

A thirst so deep that
I long for madness.
The madness that comes
from drinking saltwater and sadness.
Tears of sadness
at the corners of my eyes.
Once taut skin
crow's feet, I despise.

What use is vanity to a fugitive?

I want to look my best
in my pretty pink dress.

What a sissy princess you are, Vega!

Soulless

Council

Loyalty is a virtue.

Unquestioned loyalty is death.

This Morning

Free Verse with Internal Dialog

I woke up this morning
before the sun.
I woke up this morning
in the dark.
I took a few deep breaths and
listened to the rain spattering on the roof.
Trickling, dripping down the gutters.
Awakening to rain and cool darkness is a summertime gift.
Clouds and rain during the oppressive summer
the heat depresses and suppresses.
But the rain and the clouds and
the heaviness revives my soul.
I crave and pine for winter, but
enough of this pointless anticipation.
Opine and define, the green pines in deep snow.
No, no, no. No snow.
It is only June and
we must deal with today.
Get up,
get dressed.
Enjoy the rain
before the sun rises.
Oh, but I see the sun rising, and
I see the pink (pussy?) sky and orange and piercing white.

No, you don't wake up with pink pussy anymore.
You don't wake up with jokes and laughter anymore.
You don't wake up with her anymore.
You bloodied that, and ruined that.

Climbing above the horizon,
faster, faster, faster, chariot of the Sun.
There are no clouds and
there is no more rain.
The ground is drier than scattered desert bones,
there was never any rain, only dreams.
I have to pee, and
sometimes I write my name in the sand (snow).
But it is only June, and
I really must cease this anticipation.
How vulnerable I am
when my zipper is down.
From behind me, an
explosive cacophony of wings.
Buzzards on the roof have been disturbed
by my penis, but I was disturbed, too.
To be frightened while urinating is
an experience not to be relished.
How the bladder suffers!
There are no clouds,
it was just early and black.
There is no rain,
it was only the buzzards on the roof with talons of black.
Clickity clack clickity clack
on my roof while I dreamed.

How I loathe the summer, and
how I loathe the desert.

Gave Up

Free Verse

I don't know what it is about me
I have tried to figure it out
I have tried to self-analyze
I have tried to self-diagnose
I have tried to self-medicate

there is something about me
there is something that people do not like about me

forty years of soul searching
and I have found nothing
but recently I realized
that I have changed

perhaps it is this place
this place of nothingness and death
this desert, emotionless desert

I realized that I gave up
I gave up trying to understand
what people dislike about me

I'm not sure when I gave up
but I absolutely gave up

if people cannot accept me for who I am
then perhaps it is better for me to ignore them
I wish someone would accept me

someone
anyone

I gave up a while back
but didn't realize it until now
I can't turn back now
I can't turn back the clock
there is no reason to hate me.
but they do
(they again?)

there is no reason to hate me
I know that people don't like me
but I don't think anyone actually hates me
well, actually, they probably do
but there is no reason to hate me

it would be nice if someone hated me
at least with hate
I could know the reason
I could ask the reason
a person who hates is happy to talk
a person who hates could tell me
what is wrong with me
why people avoid me
why people pity me
why people laugh at me
why people target me

dislike is so much worse than hate
they dislike who I am
I wish they would hate me for something I have done
I wish there was a reason to dislike me

I am only myself
and I guess that's not good enough
they (they...) dislike me for who I am

hate would be less painful
hate would be relieving

Depraved

ABCB

Ring my bell,
wring my neck.

Choke me, whip me,
I'm a wreck.

Suffering

Internal Dialog

I enjoy suffering,
but this was not always the case.
I used to be normal,
but I became a mental case.

Are you sure that you used to be normal?

I used to have money
I used to have lovers
I used to host parties
I used to have friends
I used to have hobbies
I used to be happy

Used to.

When it all fell apart
I imploded like a dying star.
A black hole
spinning out of control.
Alone in the dark
a darkness thoroughly complete.
I collapsed inward and transformed
and I became a masochist.
Before I even knew the meaning of masochist
I forced deprivation upon myself.
I starved myself
and punished myself with oppressive summer heat.
No air conditioning

and no swimming pool.
For years, I have punished myself in many ways
and lived in this rotting, moldy house that sways.
Spartan, minimalist, Biblical, critical,
I shall not want.
Scraping mana from the ground
and surviving and existing.
Humbling my ego
in this rotting, moldy house that sways.

Moses.
Minus the righteousness.
Minus the leadership.
Minus the infamy.
Minus the support system.
Minus everything.

What once was a struggle, masochism,
has become an addiction.

An addiction to depravity and worthlessness.

I have not finished humbling myself.
I have not finished suppressing myself.

But you are getting close to the end.

Simp

Monostitch

You are beautiful

but annihilating.

Nice Man Redux

Internal Dialog

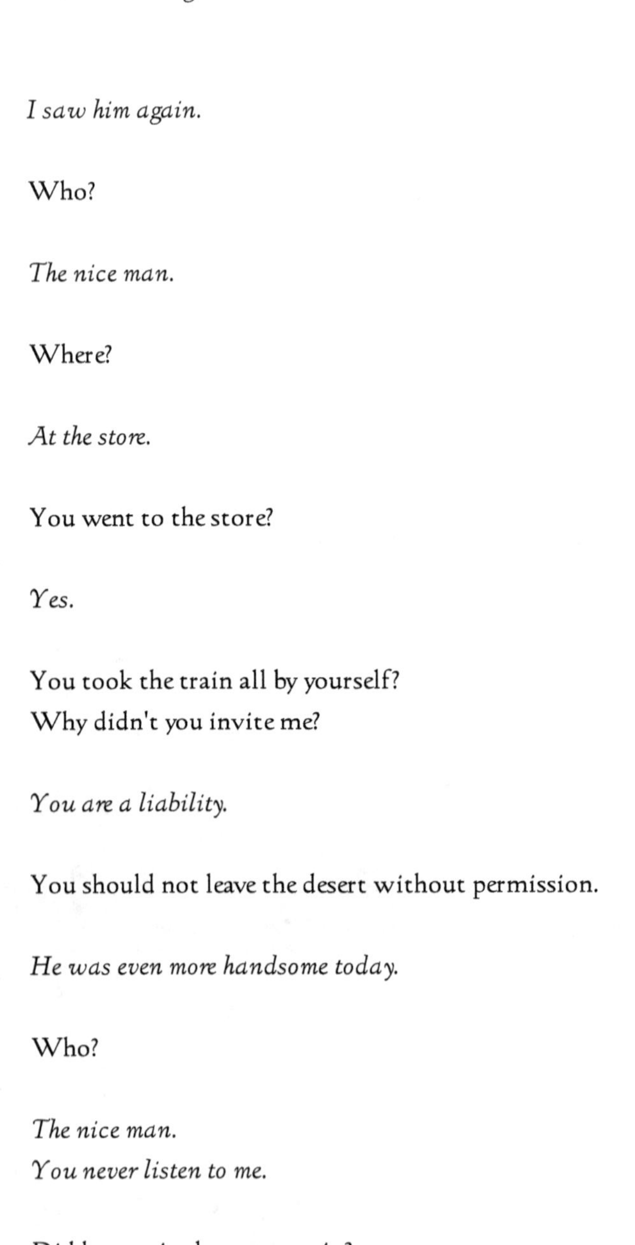

I saw him again.

Who?

The nice man.

Where?

At the store.

You went to the store?

Yes.

You took the train all by yourself?
Why didn't you invite me?

You are a liability.

You should not leave the desert without permission.

He was even more handsome today.

Who?

The nice man.
You never listen to me.

Did he manipulate you again?

No.
He ignored me.

He didn't ignore you.
He forgot you.

Why must you be so cruel?
Can I not enjoy one moment?
Can I tell you nothing of importance?
Can I share nothing of my life?

Drama Queen.

His name is Vincent.

You are not allowed to speak with him.

I didn't.
I read his name tag.

A blue-collar worker?
You are settling for a working man with a name patch?

He's a better man than you will ever be.
He's a better manipulator than you will ever be.
I can talk to whomever I wish, and
I will not talk to you for the rest of the day!

Cuddle

ABCB

come to Mommy and tell Me
whisper in My ear
flick your tongue inside Me
tell Me everything you fear

Rage

Political, Internal Dialog

Where did you get that newspaper?

I went to the store.

You went to the store?
What store?
When?

While you were sleeping.

But we are fifty miles from town.

You were asleep for a long time.

Why didn't you wake me?

You didn't wake me when you went to the store yesterday.
Then you said you would not speak to me again.
I needed some space.
You needed space, too.
We can have our own lives sometimes.

Fine.
Be grumpy.
At least tell me what you are reading about.

The older I become
the more I hate.
The older I become

the more I rage.
I hate and rage and rebel
against things I mistook for truth.
Against things I was told were truth
by people I trusted.
Russian soldiers attack, murder, rape,
but the western world says, "It's only the soldiers."
It's not the will of the people
the people are fed lies (so *they* say).
Yet the Russian people come to the western internet,
and to western software, games, news, social media.
"We don't have any information."
"We have State controlled media that lies to us."
"We are forced to be ignorant."
You are browsing western internet.
You can see news, videos, and truth with your own eyes.
Russian citizens know the truth,
but they prefer Putin's truth.
Lies are comforting,
but rape crosses a line.
Raping women and children
executing men and the elderly like they are trash.
It has meaning, right?
It has meaning to Putin and the Russian people.
It is important work, right?
Raping women and children, executing the men and the elderly.
This is very important work for Putin and the Russian people.
"We don't know what our government does."
You are browsing western internet.
Open your mind and use your brain.
See how your government suffocates freedom.
You are using western games, software, and programs.
Simply look for yourself with your own eyes and mind!

Willful ignorance is not bliss.
Willful ignorance is lying by omission.
Omitting the truth from yourself.
Lying to yourself.

The Russian people know the truth of their country,
yet the west says, “It’s only the soldiers.”
"The Russian people fund the murdering,
but the Russian people don’t do the murdering themselves."
"The Russian people are victims."
Accomplices? Guilt by association?
No, no. "We are innocent bystanders."
Therefore, the world should welcome Russian citizens.
Open arms for the willfully ignorant, lying, Russian citizens.
It is the Russian citizen who is the victim!
The murderer is the victim!
The murderer is doing the world a favor!

Ukraine is corrupt.

Genocide is Russia's gift to humanity.

the satire drips like honey
and stinks of iron(y)
and coagulates
pools of blood and honey on the ground
the murders are welcomed
their crimes ignored
if only you and I could be so ignorant and blissful
our crimes justified and swept under the rug

This is why I didn't wake you.
You force me to remember.
I want to forget.

I will never allow you to forget what you did.

Important

Political, Internal Dialog

Ah, humanity.
Paragon of importance,
of self-importance.
A species without equal,
unrivaled commanders of the Universe.
Math, science, faith.
Humanity is of the highest order.
Such grandiose equivalences!
How does humanity commission its self-proclaimed Godliness?
War.
Border fences.
Famine.
Social media.
Environmental disaster.
Abortion.
Capital punishment.
Racism.
Genocide.

Lick the satire from the knife blade,
the insipid, bloody edge.
Jagged burs remain from sharpening,
hone upon the forked tongue of humanity.
How important we are!
Jack of all,
master of none.
Self-proclaimed Godliness.
A hyper focus on one's self leads to:
Depression.

Anxiety.
Insanity.
Hopelessness.
Violence.
Murder.
Anger.
Vanity.
Delusion.
Disillusion.

Social media is the most devastating weapon ever created by humankind.
Self-importance is a plague,
humbleness is the only vaccine.
You are not important,
humanity is nothing.
Try not to be an asshole,
you are worthless and your life has no value.
Self-importance is a fallacy.
Self-importance only applies to you.
No one knows your rules or expectations.
We are all equal
when we lie in graves.
Don't be an asshole.
We are humans
and we are nothing.
Humble yourself.

Reality

Council

Anger is irrational,

but do you truly hate nothing?

Pretty Girl

Free Verse with Internal Dialog

The forest in spring is a vibrant feast for the eyes.
The angle of the sun grows more acute by the day,
showering the canopy with golden energy.
April showers bring May flowers, or so they say.
I keep running into *they*.

Who is they?
How times must I ask?
Who is they?

An expanding, exploding mushroom cloud of life.
Flowers, grasses, short trees, tall trees, shrubs, bulbs.
So much pollen, so much sperm.
So much pregnancy, so much fertility.
She always referred to herself as Fertile Myrtle.

No, just a crape myrtle.
She was right.

For many people, spring is the happiest time of year.
The time of year for new life, and
a time for reignited passion after the drogues of winter.
The frigid, heartless, unrelenting, unforgiving,
dormant, lonely, winter.

I humbly disagree with many people,
or perhaps egotistically disagree.
Spring is not happiness.
Spring is warfare.

I am not an idealist,
I am a realist.
I see things as they are,
not as they could be, nor as they should be.
Spring is conflict.
Spring is escalation.
Spring is an arms race.
Troops amass along borders throughout the winter,
spring unleashes the dogs of war.
This is not a war of patriotism,
nor a war of principles.
This is a war to the death.
A war for resources and territory,
but she would never admit to that.
After six months of quiet dormancy and dignified kinship,
neighbor turns against neighbor.
Brown grass greens,
its dormant roots resuscitated.
If the grass grows too slowly, then
it will suffocate.
Suffocate under an umbrella of weeds,
umbrella of nursing, whining saplings.
Shoots, branches, spores, limbs, pollen, seeds, sperm.
The first salvos of spring, and
the air thunders with the raining arrows of war and life.
Water drips onto the forehead of our child who wasn't to be,
as water drips onto the seeds of trees.
Tiny seeds buried in darkness,
sperm buried deep inside.
Smothered and medicated before life could begin.
Limb over limb and head over heels,
branches in hand-to-hand combat for sunlight.
Sometimes branches from a single tree will

fight amongst themselves, self-harm.
There is no camaraderie here,
no brotherhood.
It's every man for himself,
every species for itself.
Higher, wider, deeper, thicker, harder,
knotty limbs raise up and deliver their seed.
For those too old to raise up knotty limbs,
spring is a depressing reminder of years gone by.
Oak attacks sycamore,
sycamore attacks pine.
Blades of grass slice at the sky, like
a tiny army of katanas defending Japan.
The tiny katana's killing blow is shade,
blackening the sky above the other samurai.
As the great female judges of Israel conquered the ancient world,
so does one feminine plant specimen stand above all warlords.
While the men and the trees wage war,
poison ivy slithers and constricts, buries her roots amongst theirs.
She cleverly builds a symbiotic relationship,
but, in truth, the symbiosis is toxic, delusional, and one sided.
Poison ivy brings nothing to the table,
she only takes from her host's pool of resources.
While the men and trees wage a war for her affections,
she hides in the shadows and laughs in dormancy.
Poison ivy is last to unfurl her banner flag, unfurl her leaves,
she makes herself known late and vanquishes the weak.
Only the strongest, knottiest tree can satisfy
her heavy vines and heavier expectations.
She sets the men and trees to work,
defending territory, building scaffolding to support her vines.
The men and trees are proud to support her vines and her crown,
but poison ivy is not content with one host tree.
No, she slithers secretly with the tips of her vines,

and whispers slutty secrets in the ears of her neighbors.
One man, one tree is not enough for poison ivy,
one man, one tree cannot support her expectations and needs.
One gives protection, another gives resources,
another gives knotty excitement.

The men and the trees realize their situation,
but they still lust for poison ivy
and they march to war for their personal Helen of Troy.

She digs fresh roots deep amongst the roots of the victor,
this man, this tree, this sappy fool, he's just another tool.
Poison ivy continues to strangle and entangle the
hearts and minds of the losers.
She releases no man,
she unwinds from no branch.
The cool breezes of fall do not scare the men or the trees,
but poison ivy does not wait for winter.
She is the first to dormancy, and
the first to pumpkin orange, lemon yellow, and blood red.
She is the first to show her true colors, as
she chassés in her slutty fall dress and poisons the minds of men.
At the first cool breeze, poison ivy is the only color in the forest,
her insatiable ego, a bold display of confidence and dominance.
Her roots and her womb are on fire,
and her victories and pregnancies are on full display in the fall.
She is the only color,
the only fire amongst the men and the trees and the green.
After a successful summer campaign for resources and subjects,
she, and poison ivy, take their rest and enjoy their plunder.
Judge, warlord, Mistress,
she has no equals and she has no rivals.
All is fair in love and war, so they say.

They again?

Poison ivy is only doing what pretty girls do.
Pretty girls take no prisoners,
there is no quarter here.

Poison ivy and pretty girls win wars.

What Covid Stole

Free Verse with Internal Dialog

It's easy to take for granted the things we have.
It is not until we lose cherished things,
or things we did not realize we cherish,
that we feel the void of their absence and mourn their loss.

Literally, Covid diminished, destroyed,
and outright caused the deaths
of millions of people worldwide.
Health is the most important asset,
because health equates to time.
Covid stole our collective health and rolled
forward our biological clocks.
When you are healthy, it's hard to imagine ever falling ill.
When you are sick, it feels like you will never recover.

Figuratively, Covid stole many other things from us.
We lost a great deal of privacy and freedom,
children lost two years of education and companionship,
and society has become intensely paranoid and angry.
Political tribalism has always existed,
but Covid sharpened tongues to spear points.
Javelins hurl back and forth between front line squads;
how sad that we are all the same army.

We lost many restaurants, venues, and events.
We lost many fun things that will never come back.
The societal consequences of Covid will ripple
through all societies for decades.
Perhaps these will be permanent stains on western society.

Of course, the collective "we" had our issues
and problems before Covid,
but in hindsight, life was less serious and
less starched than it is today.
I am not suggesting that life before Covid wasn't serious.
Of course it was.
Life before Covid felt just as serious as any other time,
but it was a different seriousness.
It was a seriousness built upon effort, drive, and desire to improve,
but we had fun along the way.
Often playful, silly, and perhaps stupid.

That world died in 2019.
We don't have fun anymore.
There is an entire generation of young adults that have never
been to a club,
attended a live concert,
gone camping,
or simply spent a day outdoors without a phone.

Artistic freedom blossomed during Covid,
but for the wrong reasons.
Being stuck inside, alone, isolated, and quarantined.
Art became a necessary escape rather than a pursuit of passion.
Art and literature are not immune to the consequences of Covid.
I would remind the artists and writers to consider the good times.
Remember the days when you pursued art solely for the joy.

Remember when art felt free, easy, and real?
When was the last time you felt free?

Sweet

Free Verse

how sweet, the early-spring morning
the light coffee, the pink rays of sunshine
dancing across dew laden blades
of electrically vibrant, green, infant grass
bent and heavy with the
oppressive weight of a frosty
late-winter night

Astronaut

Free Verse with Epistolary

how glorious it must be
to blast off into space
a rocket ride to weightlessness
and a first-hand look at divinity
witness the heavens and circle the earth
thirteen times per day
do astronauts grieve the loss of terrestrial, pink sunrises?
dancing like marionettes as they dangle and cling
to a life so fragile in zero gravity outside of the space station
in their puffy white marshmallow suits that look comfortable
and safe like a baby in swaddling
coffins are comfortable, too
but what do they protect us from?
worms, rain, decay, filth
for a few years, anyways
until we return to the planet
the planet that launched the james webb telescope
which confirmed the first official exo-planet
i've always thought of earth as an exo-planet
well, from the alien perspective
a planet seeded by another planet
little green men
(why do aliens only have one gender?
where do i find a little green woman?)
colonizing other planets not by force
but by shooting ropey, sticky DNA all over the galaxy
they say that mushrooms and roaches can survive the vacuum of space
maybe that's how earth began
maybe that's what our DNA is built upon

nasty little fungi spores and vile nuclear-proof cockroaches
i've always had faith in aliens
their silver space suits, bald heads, and oversized anime eyes
(yes, i use the oxford comma
and yes, so should you
don't be a mouth-breathing troglodyte)
i knew they would come for me one day
little green men (women?) beam me up to their space ship
and show me live streams of you
watching you kiss and love and fuck your new guy
they ask me questions and show me things
do i want to destroy the earth
do you want to build a black hole
do you want to collapse the sun
do you want to inseminate a little green woman (they do exist!)
do you want revenge (meh, not really)
they have a big red button
one of those "easy" buttons like in the commercials
i pushed the easy button and you appeared
in my DM's
if i push it again, the earth goes away
a sniper rifle laser beam photon torpedo blast from heaven
they named the weapon "the end of suffering"
(for three years, i have been asking who is 'they'
as for now, i have not received a response)
i'm sadistic but i'm not a murderer
do you know that the sixth commandment is mistranslated?
king james ['s sycophants] translated it as “thou shall not kill”
i wonder if the error was intentional
regardless, the proper translation from hebrew is
“thou shall not murder”
the difference being that murder is illegal killing
some killing is legal, you see?
i would rather watch you suffer

or is it i who suffers?
while i watch you on the big screen monitor
like captain kirk watching your husband does a ryker move on your pussy
(i still don't understand why you refused to treat your yeast infection
six years later, and my fingers still smell like a fucking fish market)
running around with your kids
(spock is still alive, by the way
and possibly elvis, too)
that you made with someone else
your diamond wedding ring glittering in the bright summer sunshine
a little rock worth more than my entire life
blinking brightly like a lost hiker signaling SOS
with a flashlight to a passing search plane
vega starlight goes blink blink blink
have you read contact?
aliens from vega, man!
vegans
but i'll not rescue you from your domestic decisions
nor from your reckless, rancid relations
is this just my masochism is kicking in?
i am no god
remember, i am no murderer either
gods kill, but they do not murder
can we finally get that straight?
i'll not push the big red easy button
seven billion people and seven billion sunsets per day
but really, who watches sunsets anymore?
it's probably more like a million sunsets per day
the poets, the artists, the aliens, the idealists,
the hopeless romantics, the existentialists,
and the people who remember a world before mobile phones
people who don't know (and don't care)
about anything higher than themselves
the self has become god

the self is killing itself
slowly, one selfie at a time
and in this, narcissism and self-importance reign supreme
social media is the new church
on your knees, it's time to worship
you're a slave to a lifestyle that you profess to hate
i remember all the things you said
how you would never end up like this
how it sickened you to think of it
i know you are suffering inside
suffering in silence because you dare not tell your husband
that you hate him, your life, and everything you have built together
you built an entire life based on a lie
but in your wake, a thousand drowning sailors
choking for breath in the horizon-less ocean of storms
waterspouts, hurricanes, and tsunamis
crash over their capsized boats
one lie after another
i'll not put you out of your misery with my heavenly weapon
i'll not rescue you
i'll not respond to your calls and texts
you can suffer just like i do
suffered every day since you left
sunset after sunset after sunset after sunset

Soft

Free Verse with Internal Dialog

Why are you single?

I don't know.

What are you looking for?

I don't know.

What do you want?

I don't know,
but I know what I don't want.

What don't you want?

I don't want to spend another night sitting around
this disgraceful, dank, moldy, filthy little apartment
chain smoking cigarettes, drinking stale black coffee,
and quoting Shakespeare back and forth with my id.

For years, these have been my lame responses
to my own lame questions.
Clueless, aimless, pointless responses.
Years of being alone.
Alone in relationships, alone single.
Same difference, the pain is the same.
The numbness is the same.
I take that back - alone while in a relationship is worse.
Loving someone who doesn't love you,

but they take from you, nonetheless.
And you are so dependent and worthless,
than you make a conscious decision to endure the abuse.

Alone in my lame office cubicle.
Alone in my lame car.
Alone in my lame apartment.
Alone in my lame life
Until last night.
Last night changed everything.
Last night, I fell in love
with the love of my life
and the ire of my life.

Last night, I found my wife.

I rarely go out anymore.
But last night, I went out.

To celebrate?

No.

With friends?

No.
Just me.

I went to a dance club.
A typical dance club.
Pink and purple lighting,
concrete floors,
strobe lights,
mirror balls,

cocktail tables,
standing room only.

I swallowed half a pill,
and swayed on the dance floor.
Bumping hips and copping feels.
Laughing at the thirsty Chads...
...those drunken, flailing, clapping seals.
Likely clapping each other's cheeks at last call.

But this dance club has a secret,
a poorly kept secret.
The dance club is only half of the building.
The back of the building is a different club entirely.
A sex club.
A *members-only* sex club.
I have been a member for a decade,
but I cannot recall the last time I was here.
Two years at least.
Before I met my previous mistake (you).

Through the black curtains and past the bouncer.
Out of the sparkle and glitter
and into the black.
In the sex club, the walls are black.
The couches are black, the rugs are black,
the leather is black, the cages are black.
Even the light is black.
Black lights hum and radiate their purplish, alien glow.
Cocktail waitresses delicately click their needle stilettos
across the painted black concrete floor.
Labia exposed and dangling between
dainty, knotted ropes of fishnet lace.

I choose a couch and lay back.
I make myself comfortable.
A cocktail waitress sits in my lap.
She takes my drink order and lights the candles on my table.
She arches her back and bulges her little belly,
her hips press down and her exposed pussy
leaves a little white, wet stain down my thigh.
Like an exclamation point of some other man's cum
blended with her inevitable gonorrhea.
Something for the black light to highlight.
No, I shouldn't say that about a working girl.
I'm sure she behaves herself.
I'm sure she is clean, and fresh, and would never do anything
to hurt me or deceive me.
She clacks away on the needle stilettos
putting on an intentional show as she goes.

And then something happened.
Something I cannot explain.
While I was watching her ass bounce,
oblivious and distracted,
a girl sat next to me on my black couch.
I looked over to her.
We did not speak.
We just stared at each other,
studied each other.
What I felt for her was not lust
but an overwhelming calmness.
Like everything was ok with the world,
and that tragedy and sadness could ever touch us.
I embraced her and she clung tightly.
Her slender, weak arms slung around my neck.
We shifted to a laying position.
Face to face, lips to lips, chest to breast.

I hugged her closely,
she held me softly, maternally.
I lost my face in her hair.
Strawberries.
I daydream of us walking hand in hand
through the late summer strawberry fields.
I wonder if her pussy smells like strawberries, too.
Strawberries and cream.
She is dressed in black.
Tiny, soft black shorts.
The bottom cut so high that her ass is exposed,
the top cut so high that her belly button is hidden
Black tube top squeezing her perky, innocent, small breasts.
Black choker.
Black earrings.
Black eyeshadow.
Black thigh-high stockings.
Black, strappy sex shoes.

I lay my face on her breasts
with my lips slightly parted and a firm nipple slipping between.
Nurse me, Mommy.

I'm only eighteen.
I am young enough to be your daughter.
May I call you Daddy?

I could sleep here indefinitely.
Every night for the rest of my life.
Her sharp little nipple presses deeper between my lips,
further back on my tongue.
Her sharp, black glitter nails drag slowly through my hair.
She is not wearing a bra,
she doesn't need one.

I love strappy sex shoes.
One finger inside.
Two fingers inside.
She is going to cum.
Three fingers inside.
Too many.
Two fingers inside.
Her body writhes and flexes.
Struggles.
Weeps and whimpers and
squirts.

The waitress returns with my drink.
The waitress gets on her knees in front of the couch.
I faintly smile,
just the corner of my mouth,
but it's enough permission for the waitress.
She puts her mouth to the soft girl's throbbing, swollen pussy.
I push my fingers deeper
while the waitress sucks her clit
and slips her tongue between my fingers.
She is cumming now.
Again.
Harder than the first time.
I squeeze her neck to muffle her voice,
but it's too late.
The entire club is watching us now.
I don't mind.
In hindsight, I like to be watched.

She runs naked to the restroom to clean herself.
Black, strappy sex shoes clicking across the concrete floor.
Hands and arms dainty and flailing,
shorts in one hand, top in the other hand.

Hair bouncing halfway down her lean back.
Saliva and cum dripping down her slender inner thighs.

She doesn't come back.
I have walked the club floor twice.
No sign of her, she is gone.
I don't even know her name.
The name of my wife.
The name of the girl who could fix my life.
I love her,
but she is gone.

My heart is crushed and bleeding out
on this black couch and black floor under the black light.

But the cocktail waitress wants more.
Wants a bigger tip.
Her lips still taste of strawberry cream.
I fuck the waitress.
The entire club is still watching.
I scan the faces for my soft girl,
for my tiny little wife,
but I see only lust and need.
My heart is broken,
but I fucked the waitress regardless.
Fucked away the pain.

Another pill for pain.
A whole pill this time.

The half-life is quick.
I'm hurting again.
Walking home at two-thirty in the morning.
Soaked from rain,

soaked from tears
soaked from cum

.

I will see her again,
but not in this life.
We are soul mates,
but not in this life.

I open my eyes.
I wake up.
It is morning and the dream has concluded.
My soft girl is gone.
She lives in another world.
A dream world.
A nightmare world of black floors and black furniture.
A world that smells of strawberries and tastes of cream.

She exists,
but not in my world.
I hate this world,
I hate my life.
This world of strife,
devoid of happiness.
Devoid of my wife.

Two pills.
Three pills.
Four pills.
Five pills.
Maybe if I swallow enough pills,
I can find my soft girl in eternity.

I don't know her name,
but I love her.

She is my wife,
in this life or the next.

Or maybe she was just a slutty wet dream.

No.
She was real.
I eventually forgot about her,
until a few months later when the doctor asked me,

Have you been having sex with prostitutes?

No, only in dreams.
Just a girl I met in a club a few months ago.
It was only once.

Creatures

Ballad

Over the hill,
it comes fumbling.
"A hint of rain,"
it says, mumbling.

As the temperature drops,
the wind begins to blow.
The cloud becomes dark.
Creatures, stay low!

Clash! Crash!
The cloud turns violent.
A tornado sprouts,
the cloud is no longer silent.

Trees topple,
flood rushes in.
I flee!
To my warm and cozy den.

Clouds are unpredictable!

Bunny, Danger!

Epistolary

Your insatiable compulsion to write poetry
is derived from your tendencies
to lie, exaggerate, and criticize others
from a high point.

No.
Trust me; it's from a low point.

Your insatiable compulsion to contact, insult, and embarrass
me is derived from your tendencies
to lie, exaggerate, and criticize others
from a high point of delusional narcissism that is validated
by a bank account that exists only in your web of uninstantiated lies.

You take, and harm, and berate,
then you blame your victim and laugh.

I do have one thing to thank you for, however;
you showed me that narcissists,
real, clinical, textbook narcissists,
don't have the ability to look in the mirror
and are incapable of understanding themselves, their words, their actions,
or the resulting pain they inflict on those around them.

For this, I forgive you.
I forgive you because I feel sorry for you.
Your life is a web of lies,
riotous, blatant lies.
When the web burns,

you will fall.
(I'm skulking down your door-less hall.)
But even as you fall, you will be spinning
and weaving more lies and avoiding the mirror,
avoiding your atrocious reflection.
Like Alice tumbling down the rabbit hole,
unaware that she is the cause of her own, strange demise.
Killing her own soul slowly
for the glorification of ego
and for attention built on lies.

Thank you for teaching me the red flags of an abuser.

Experiment

Ballad

Through the gate,
creatures lurk.
Claiming my mind,
forever lost.

Crouching low,
in an alley of darkness.
Its claws, unsheathed,
incomparable to the rest.

It's ready to pounce
on my quivering soul.
As it slinks closer
like a wolf towards a foal.

My eyes flinch and
the beast springs upon me.
It stands on my chest,
and it shows no mercy.

A bright light appears
as I gasp a last breath.
Toward the creature I veer;
this is death.

On my way up
I hear someone say,
"The project was a success.
Good day, fellow doctors, good day!"

Truth

Council

Always trust a person who is seeking truth.

Never trust a person who has found truth.

\apocalypse.exe\

Shakespearean Sonnet

Defiant dandelion dredges deep,
a concrete crack for roots to call a home.
Dystopian winter inspires sleep,
but dandelion blooms a yellow crown.

Overgrown sidewalk, no treading feet.
Nuclear fallout extinguished life.
Dandelion and cockroach compete
for territory guarded from the strife.

Acid rain and ash-blackened skies
make smudged glass buildings cry mascara tears.
Humanity at war did cause to die
all life. Extinct is the emotion of fear.

Robots and AI now rule the Earth.
Will God return to validate man's worth?

We Lost Our Way

Poet's Prose

Lost in the Utah canyon lands; a misanthropic horseback ride gone south. The dry winter winds chase the sun's mocking face and its last remaining blushes from the sky; night falls on the geriatric, wrinkled knuckles of the land. As the earth rotates her head for a better view of the canyons, the setting sun is replaced by the rising of a razor blade sliver of moon; trading atavistic laughing for dim foreboding. The blank canyons whistle and hum and chant and drum, playing tricks on the mind; leftover curses from long-dead civilizations like a wispy hand unintentionally passing in front of the lens and haunting the long-exposure of an otherwise sharply focused and contrasted night photograph. Tiny red desert strawberries are tempting, but they are hallucinogenic and rather insipid; the poison slithers down my throat, and Butch Cassidy and his Wild Bunch go galloping by as they return to their secret hideout, cartoon burlap sacks with dollar signs printed on the side are flopping in tow. My horse breaks its lead and escapes; the galloping beat of a native chief riding the canyon floor and painting the walls red with blood. Dew drops condense and parachute from the air onto syringe needles of cacti; the gently falling tears of abused civilizations who cry out for reparation, but the scales of justice decline to hear the case. The campfire is petite and efficient, and its flickering light throws wavering, dancing shadows on the canyon walls; this is the reparation, this is the payback, this is the curse.

Loneliness, thirst, panic, hunger.

Unknown Mailing Address

Epistolary

My mother cleaned her attic
then she gave me a box
full of ancient grade-school papers, photos, and knick-knacks.
Generally, I enjoy reminiscing and remembering,
but I must be forthright that some of the items in the box
are beyond embarrassing and venture into the realm
of regret, of cringe, of failure, and of self-loathing.
It is unfair, with the benefit of hindsight, to judge
my young self for being awkward, lame, and ignorant;
although, I still embody these things in abundance
in adulthood, and thus, I shouldn't find myself surprised.
The love notes are always the worst.
They make my heart sad and cause my chalice
of emotions to runeth over with guilt.
Guilt, not only for failing to convince
any girl that I was worth her time,
but also guilt for wasting
the time of so many intelligent, gorgeous, hopeful young women.
High quality girls who just wanted to talk to me,
just wanted to know me and be friendly, as girls do.
In my own mind, I twisted generic kindness into genuine interest.
They were not interested, they were just being friendly.
I was so far behind in social development that I couldn't tell
the difference between a friend and a crush.
Even now on the brink of 40 years,
I cannot tell the difference between customer service and flirtation.
You call me a misogynist.
No, it is not true.
Your perception of misogyny is simply a misunderstanding

and a predictable result of liberal, public-school brainwashing.
Hunting social injustices where none exist.
I misunderstand women
and you misunderstand me.
Don't you see?
I am the proverbial Gen X.
The proverbial 'Lost Generation.'
I would love nothing more than to pick up a pen and paper and write
a letter to you. A long letter, a twenty-page letter.
But would you read it?
Would you open your mailbox and take me seriously?
Or throw me away with the junk mail and go right back to your phone
and your tiktok and your attention and your envy.
I'm a good person.
Do you know how I know that?
Because I hate myself. Because I feel guilty.
Do you hate yourself? Do you feel guilty?
No, you don't.
Because you're not a good person.
And the world is dominated by bad people.
People who feel no guilt, no self-hatred, no remorse.
What you perceive as -all of the - liberal trigger words
is just gas-lighting.
If we wrote letters back and forth
snail mail,
for a decade,
then my epistolary form would improve,
and so would yours.
Perhaps we could even come to an understanding or
a mutual respect.
The problem is that people no longer take the time
to understand each other.
It's no longer a forced exercise.
What are you going to do with a piece of paper,

a candle, a pen, and a friend,
in the middle of the night?
You learn about each other, you talk,
you record poetic ideals honed by tea and tobacco.
I wish people would come to my house for dinner,
sit around the table with food, pens, a fresh deck of cards,
and stack of clean paper.
We would read English novels, and Russian novels,
and poetry from all over the world,
and drink Popcorn Sutton's moonshine.

I want my life to be an epistolary.
But to whom do I address the letter?
Who will sit with me, and debate me,
and think of ways to improve the world?
I tell you, I read Jane Austen and my heart dies.
The tragedy of humanity is that the more advanced we become,
the more we fail one another as human beings.

My epistolary form is maturing.
Please, may I forward just one more letter?

It is often said that the definition of 'depression' is
"Living in the past."

So, no.
I will not write any more letters.
I will leave behind no more remnants
of confused and embarrassing memories.

My epistolary form has matured,
but I want to be a photographer instead.
A photographer of sadness, and beauty, and wrinkles, and freckles.

Free portraits!
I'll be here all week.

Or, likely, the rest of my life.

Deck Chair

Free Verse with Internal Dialog

I should probably buy a new deck chair,
but you know how we libertines are.
We run things ragged,
and we use things hard until there is nothing left.
My deck chair one of those cheap, aluminum, fold-out chairs.
The kind with the plaid straps that creak, pop, and fray.
When you sit down too hard in one of these old plaid chairs
your ass breaks through to the ground,
and your knees get pinned to your face
(not that you have ever minded such circumstances).
One of those

plaid-strapped-aluminum-frame-folding-deck-chairs.

She still has some grip,
still has some pliability.
Her walls are not what they used to be,
because I have stretched them over the years.
Her fleshly little wings no longer flap and quiver.
I'm too wide, too girthy.
Sat down too quickly,
laid into her hard one too many times.
I take responsibility for the loosening
of her stitching.
But I'll not claim her fraying.
She did that all on her own.

When I say deck, I do not mean porch.
A porch has a roof and is part of the house.

A deck is a large, raised, wooden structure
which is commonly used for entertaining.

It is upon this deck that sits my

plaid-strapped-aluminum-frame-folding-deck-chair

and upon this chair sits me.

Twelve months per year.
Four seasons per year.
I see it all, and the

plaid-strapped-aluminum-frame-folding-deck-chair

sees it all.
Scorching heat, windy fall, icy winter, wet spring.

I like to sit with my legs crossed,
one over the other.
It makes me feel academic and wise,
self-validated and worthy of philosophical thought.
My legs make a nice table for my steno pad.
Who needs an office when you have a

plaid-strapped-aluminum-frame-folding-deck-chair.

Here I sit with my morning coffee
and watch the sun rise over the trees.
Here I sit with iced tea and a cucumber sandwich
and hide under the matching plaid umbrella
during the heat of summer afternoons.
Here I sit with fatty meats
grilling, smoking, blackening, rendering,

preparing, plating, and serving

carcinogens.

I love to sit in my

plaid-strapped-aluminum-frame-folding-deck-chair

while the grill wisps and hisses.
Sometimes I read a book while I grill.
Sometimes I get piss drunk on vodka, smoke cigarettes,
and ignore every responsibility of life.
Wife and kids, obviously...
Fuck.
Why did I get married?
I don't even like kids.
My ashtray of feigned ignorance.
My ashtray of regret and reclusiveness.

Fuck.

An orange, dusty, fall afternoon.
My favorite weather.
One hour remains of daylight,
one hour until sunset.
The grill is heating up, coming to temperature.
It is cool outside but there is still enough summer
left in the air such that I do not need a jacket.

My favorite aspect of fall on the deck in my
plaid-strapped-aluminum-frame-folding-deck-chair
is being surrounded by the fruits of my labor.
No, I do not mean my wife and children.

Dependent, snot-nosed, little leaches.

I mean my blood, sweat, and tears.
My plants, my babies.
I cultivate and surround myself with containers full of plants.
Tall plants, short plants,
plants with beans and seeds and pods and flowers and fruits.
There are so many plants on the deck
that I must blaze and maintain a proper trail.
Have you ever picked a vegetable from a plant that you
grew from seed, and placed it directly on the grill?
Having been separated from its mother for mere moments
before being julienned, oiled, salted, and charred.

Fresh babies for dinner.

Eggplant is an exquisite example:
Sever the umbilical cord,
get a good first and last look at the plump flesh,
fillet the skin back and expose the fatty tissues,
cut into evenly sized pieces,
oil liberally (extra virgin),
salt, pepper, garlic,
grill on high heat until char marks are severe
and flesh is tender yet retains some firmness.

The back door is open.
I yell through the open door to my wife
and ask her if the steaks are ready for the grill.
Her smut reality show is turned up too loud
so I have to yell again
from my

plaid-strapped-aluminum-frame-folding-deck-chair.

It's one of those shows where the wives all hate each other,
and try to fuck each other's husbands,
but manage to be civil long enough to film an episode.

My wife hates me.
She has never indicated this with words,
but a mindful, watchful husband can sense these things.
Just like my

plaid-strapped-aluminum-frame-folding-deck-chair,

my wife is frayed and fragile
and loose
and riddled with osteoporosis
and several other diseases of the geriatric woman.

Twenty years of kinks and childbirths
have run her pussy into the ground,
have run her mind ragged into the unsound.

She finally yells back:
Yes, dear.
The steaks are almost ready.
Please allow a few more minutes
for them to come up to room temperature.
I love you!
Can I get you another drink?

She should have set the steaks out an hour ago.
Worthless.
Whatever.
More time for vodka,

writing philosophy about the legitimacy of aliens,
and filleting eggplant skin.

I grow other things, too.
On the shady side of the deck,
I grow the more delicate plants in orange clay containers.
Leafy plants,
pointy plants,
sensitive plants,
special plants.

From left to right:
salvia
basil
peyote
rosemary
castor bean
dill
water hemlock
bay leaf
oleander
oregano
nightshade

A few years back,
my wife and I vacationed in Greenland.
I brought back a mortar and pestle as a souvenir.
The salesman claimed the mortal and pestle were carved from
a rare piece of igneous rock that was formed underwater.
It looks like plain-old-ordinary granite to me.

Wife again:
Would you mind seasoning the steaks like you did last time?

If you turned down the smut,
you wouldn't have to yell.
Shrill bitch.

I would be happy to grind some fresh seasonings for your steak.
Just like last time,
and the time before that,
and the time before that,
and the time before that.
I know how much you love my homegrown seasonings.

I slip on a latex glove, interlock my fingers, and flex.
I clip a few of the castor beans.
I grind the beans with the mystical mortar and pestle.
I grind until I reach a fine powder consistency.
I liberally rub my special seasoning into the steaks.
But not my steak,
never my steak.
I'm careful to label my steak.
No mistakes.

The special seasoning is only for my wife and kids.

Olive Tree

Free Verse

Suffocating in the heavy rains and muddy drippings
of the ceaseless storm above my head where thunderheads
and severed heads of men roll and spill
their blood upon to the soil
into the soil and through the roots of this olive tree
the rain and blood
mixes into mud
and sloshes upon my head
down here, entangle in the olive tree roots.

Look down.
Keep your head down and mouth open
to get a breath of the dank, black, wet air
air that is completely devoid of oxygen
or the life that men need to survive
but trees plunge their roots happily into this life
and thrive despite the bloody humanity
happening all around them.

As does the cock crow and banish the Ghost
so do the clutching fingers of the dead
sow shackles to my ankles
and pull me back down below
where the rising sun shall never touch
my rotting face again for all eternity.

Kings and Queens, Presidents, Czars, and Commanders
stand on the backs of slaves and soldiers and commoners
and the fine minutiae of variable servantry padding barefoot

or steel-boot-clad and on their knees before the
Kings and Queens, Presidents, Czars, and Commanders
begging to be sent to war, begging to be sent to death,
begging to be sent to the blackness and the deeply rooted,
muddy, prison cell under the olive tree
an olive tree intended for peace
planted with loved and cherished
idolized upon this hallowed hill
an ancient, historic hill with deep roots
and deep soil full of arms
and legs and skulls
an olive tree planted along the border of two countries
along the border of sanity and insanity
but which is which, no man living or dead can say
only the olive tree can say
she whispers and wails of the banished and regretful dead
men lying among her rooted feet and legs
gratefully dead soldiers who need only to look up
into her bosom, her fruit is plentiful and juicy

2am

Free Verse

2am
my eyes hurt
staring at the ceiling fan
avoiding thoughts
avoiding anything real
trying to be numb
round and round we go
another night of staring at the ceiling fan
sometimes i stare for so long that i get dizzy
not like ring-around-the-rosey dizzy
but medically dizzy
sometimes it makes me vomit
i once tried to get out of bed and collapsed
laid out
fell out
dizzy on the floor
i really need a new 2am hobby

Manly

Free Verse

What is a man if not a man?
Clothing, actions, words, and work.
What is a man who walks a different path?
In the eyes of society, he is nothing.
If a man rejects the things which society defines as man,
then what has the man become?
Perhaps it could be argued that he is a renegade.
Perhaps it could be argued that he is a pioneer.
Or an entrepreneur.
Or unemployed.
Or homeless.
Or a starving artist.
Real men sit in office chairs sixty hours per week.
Providing for the family they created,
the family they ignore under the guise of "busy" and "work."
Don't worry, his wife is getting plenty of attention.
What is a man if not a man?
A man in a man-made prison.
Is that a man?
When was it decided that money determines worth?
A man is only a man if his bank account is six inches or better.
Let's be honest, his penis is irrelevant.
If a man and his penis are irrelevant,
if a man and his passions are vagrants,
is he still a man?
If not a man, then what?
A boy in man's clothing?
Men are slaves to the democratic capitalist system.
Lithium batteries who fuel the very social change

that seeks to destroy masculinity and manliness.
Want to change politics?
Want to change society?
Quit your job, quit paying taxes, take back your penis.
Society will be so angry about your manliness!
The feminists will be so angry about their loss of income!
Force them to divorce from their government daddy.
Just retire so you can stop paying taxes.
I won't hold my breath waiting for the feminists to fill
jobs like plumber, bricklayer, heavy equipment operator.
How easy is it to complain that there are not enough women
in corporate America.
You know why there are less women in corporate America?
Because it's a shitty life.
Most men are not even willing to sacrifice everything to be C-Suite.
The minuscule fraction of men who are even qualified
is a needle in a haystack.
Don't you understand how cold and dead inside they must feel?
What woman would want that for herself and her family?
Why don't you want the same equality in bricklaying?
If equality in all things in the goal,
what is stopping you?
Why do you need men to help you?
If women wanted to take over the bricklaying industry,
they could start today.
But they don't.
Because it's not about equality.
It's about assaulting men.
But what the feminists don't realize is that men don't need women.
Deny it all you like, but women need men.
You will never build a house, design a car,
vacuum a truck-full of shit out of a broken septic tank.
The problem with feminism is that it removes responsibility
from women and puts it on men.

Universities are 65% women, a statistic that is accelerating quickly.
Women are smarter, more diligent,
more dedicated, more serious.
So then why is the C-Suite predominantly male?
Because women eventually realize they don't want to sacrifice
their entire lives in favor of work.
Why is this the fault of men?
No one is stopping you from obtaining an MBA
and getting hired by a publicly traded corporation.
No one is stopping you from working your way up to the C-Suite.
No one is stopping you from being a truck driver, farmer, or carpenter.
Why does having a penis mean that I am suppressing your ability
to apply for the jobs you want?
Feminism (and other contemporary social justice movements)
are successful because they remove the need for personal responsibility.
You get to play the victim.
Your decisions are someone else's fault,
and that is powerfully addictive marketing message.
Unfortunately, it's not true.
Feminism hurts women, not men.
We will be just fine without you.
Take responsibility for your own decisions.
If you don't like your life, then change it.
Don't blame a CEO as your reason for dropping out of college.
And what about these men dressing as women
and taking over every aspect of female life.
Do you want your daughter competing in sports against
a woman who has her penis tucked between her legs?
Where are the feminists now?
There are wolves in sheep clothing infiltrating your defenses,
but you blame men.
Blame yourselves.
This is the culture you created.
This is the culture you encourage.

You think it is men who are under assault, but you are wrong.
Men will be just fine.
Maybe we have to be single because there are fewer and fewer rational women to date, but single is better than unhappy.
Men will be just fine.
Feminism is destroying women, and the more obvious the pain becomes, the deeper the feminists dig in.
The more they shift blame.
The more they disassociate from personal responsibility.

So I will go to Mars on an Elon Musk starship.
Build my own little greenhouse on the rusty ground
with the 1% atmosphere.
I'll be a fish out of water,
I'll be a Martian florist.
I'll be just fine without you.

I Know

Free Verse

Stop saying, "I know."
"I know" equates to "fuck you."
If your narcissism cannot resist responding, then say, "You're right."
When you say "I know," what you are actually doing is
stopping the conversation,
because you have reached a point where you are so
uncomfortable and frustrated with your lack
of knowledge that all you have left to say is "I know."
No, you don't "know."
If you did "know," you wouldn't be saying "I know"
to a person who knows more than you;
a person who is just trying to help you improve.
"I know."
No.
You don't fucking know,
and you just convinced me to give up on you.
"I know" you better than you know yourself.
Fuck you, too.

Lucky

Epistolary

I don't think about you anymore.
I wonder if that means I don't love you anymore?
No, that is not the truth.
I still love you, but I don't think about you anymore.
Not in the present sense, at least.
I think about the time I spent with you
and the bad decisions I regretfully made.
I think about you traveling around the world with your husband.
I don't think about you, per say,
but you still find ways to slither into my thoughts.
The other day, I pulled a book from my shelf
that I hadn't read in years. A heavy, thick reference book
to keep me company at breakfast.
Out of the book, you fell.
Well, not you per say.
Just your memory.
No, our memory.
One that we shared.
Out of the book fell a folded piece of wax paper.
Inside of the paper were several perfectly pressed four leaf clovers.
You always claimed to be the best at finding four leaf clovers.
You always claimed to have a divinely-gifted sixth sense of luck.
I wonder if you noticed how much I enjoyed standing over you
while you crawled around the yard on your hands and knees?
You asked me if could accept love, if I could accept your love, and
I replied no.
I loved you, but I couldn't accept love - yours or otherwise.
I knew that by accepting your love I would be accepting permanence.
I wasn't ready for permanence.

I can tell you honestly that rejecting your permanence
was the biggest mistake of my life.
Watching you walk away will haunt me forever.
I don't think about you anymore,
but I do wonder about the what-if's.

Pressure

Free Verse

pressure induces creativity
time pressure
money pressure
desperate situations yield the quickest results
desperation yields intensity
a pressure cooker filled with ball bearings
set to detonate and rip apart feet and legs
shrapnel rips away the appendages that anchored
you like concrete for so long

pressure induces creativity,
but not in the way you are probably assuming
pressure equates to responsibility
it is responsibility that induces my creativity

i loathe responsibility
i avoid it until it causes enough tension, that if it were to snap,
london bridge is falling down
that would be a colossal responsibility

i deal with responsibility only when it is evident that failing
to do so would result in increased responsibility

the alarm clock
responsibility on a pedestal
the alarm clock, apex predator
preying on joy
i hide from the talons of responsibility
down in the weeds, i hide

and i write
and i paint
and i pretend...

...i pretend like this is fun

Shell

Free Verse

emerging from the bleak and altogether too well known
spaces of my regretful one bedroom home
it's cold outside but i don't care
the sea oats with this dead and dormant heads
smack into each other in the frigid wind
like an audience clapping for the main character
as they pull the curtain aside on opening light
a stripper pulling her panties aside on ladies night
barefoot and hopeful, toes and heels sink into the watery sand
as a wave pulls away. i wonder what parts of me have been pulled
away into the vastness of an ocean. salt is hellbent
on dissolving even the most vile of trash,
a fat little hermit crab tumbles back and forth with the wash
then i realize that it is dead
morbidity and curiosity grip me and i find a little stick to pry the crab
out of its shell, out of its home
(i wonder if crab shells collect cobwebs in the little
spiral corners that their soft, strange bodies cannot reach?)
shells are ghosts,
haunted, abandoned houses
like when you move into a new apartment and you can smell
the skin flakes and the memories of the people who just moved out
the crab won't budge, it's stuck
petrified literally and metaphorically
maybe it refused to leave
refused to brave the world and accept change
but forgot to stop eating
and grew lazy and heavy and depressed
and fatter and fatter

and tighter in it's juvenile shell
surrendering to the inevitable fate that time does not stop
comfortable isn't really comfortable at all
responsibility is uncomfortable
fuck being an adult
refusing to move on is akin to suicide

self-inflicted homicide of the soul

Umbrella

Concrete Poem

rain
falls pitter patter
umbrella takes a sighing breath
stretches its ribs and pulls apart its fleshy fabric
like a frilled lizard throwing open its paper tiger shield
the dominating winter wind overpowers, umbrella turns to parachute
inside out and upside down, stumble backwards into a puddle and nearly fall down
down down it falls in front of a big glass window of a coffee and sandwich shop full of eyes
bursting through the door is a knight in shining armor in full reveille and giddy laughter to help
reign in the umbrella and quell the raging storms of embarrassment and disdain for winter rain

and now you call him husband and grip tight to him when the cold rain falls
and winter
rages inside you

Forty-Seven Candles

Free Verse

One after the other on my mantle
above the sickly, yellow fire
one candle for each failed loved
a menorah of crushed hearts
the tallest and center-most candle is my own
always red, always a trick candle that never goes out
even when spit upon, it sparks back to life
ready to be embarrassed again and again
forty seven dripping, crying candles
tears pooling and cooling into stalagmites of bitter memories
arguments, last words, mutual hatreds, rejections, and relegations
(don't forget the oxford comma)
a wax museum of dead relationships
stand behind the velvet rope
the tour starts here
i'll be your host and guide on today's foray into the past
follow me and gaze upon the waxy likenesses of those i loved and lost
walk the black and white marble floor
the maze of beauty and desperation
turn your attention here (points down, palm open)
this is where my bloody knees dragged across the grout
and left a trail of red up to the feet of her (hand points up)
her greasy, shiny face and defeated, tired eyes
too much make up and not enough sleep
follow me! everyone
listen how your feet pop on the marble floor
and echo through the maze of time
but this game has no end, no goal, no victor
the echo sounds like someone is following just behind

smelling your sweat and fear, whispering words too soft to understand
camouflaged and hidden in the blackness of your shadow
when you stop, their feet stop too
stalking behind you instead of walking beside you
hand in hand like a lover
would you like to hold her hand?
kneel and look up at her?
any volunteers? (two hands up, palms up, held steady, then question)
run your fingers gently over her lips
her strong cheekbones, her square jaw, her severe nose
what a pleasure to be under her waxy, meaty pussy
to serve and slave and support and clean and fuck and cum
mind the puddles, dears
the roof is leaking
pick a wax statue and wrap your arm around their shoulders
or poke your head between their thighs
if you ask nicely, they may even stand on your hands
so their wax feet will never touch the filthy floor
group photo packages are available in the lobby
smile! cheese!

Fall Rut

Haiku

buck trance-walks soy beans
antlers and nose high, dumb doe
poacher kills my view

Divine

Political Ballad

divining rod
witching stick
poke and prod
water wicked

call FEMA
no one home
pete buttigieg
a garden gnome

drink the water
you'll be fine
norfolk southern
taxpayer dime

poison spell
time to move
wishing well
oily sheen, please excuse

Smoke Show

Free Verse

I repeat the same wind-down every evening.
Some might call that a routine,
but I prefer to think of it as a ritual.
A hot bath fixes just about everything
that is wrong with the world.
I like to pour a glass of red wine
and fill the glass until it's almost overflowing.
I never drink white wine in the bathtub,
I never drink white wine anywhere, actually.
White wine is for old women at fancy parties.
Socialites with something to prove
to themselves and to each other.
I'm a red wine girl and I'll always be a red wine girl.
I have a little wooden table beside the tub
where the glass of red wine waits with bated breath.
I love my smut novels.
Another guilty pleasure on a long list
of guilty pleasures.
I figure that if I am already wet and slippery in the tub,
then I may as well get a little more wet and slippery.
The book goes on the tub-side table, too.
The tub is full, bubbly, and steamy.
Squeaky is the cog that turns the water off.
Drip, drip, drip go the last droplets.
Have I mentioned how much I hate fluorescent lights?
You know the type of lights that I mean.
Those terrible office building lights that burn your retinas,
and burn your soul until your passions and dreams
are nothing more than a smoldering, black heap of ashes.

I turn off all of the unholy lights in the entire house.
In the bathtub, I read by candlelight,
two candles, in fact.
It is pitch black otherwise.
Bone black with a dab of phthalo blue.
I like the scented, girlie candles,
but I have to be careful when I light two.
The scents can easily clash.
One blueberry, one vanilla.
This smells like the most amazing ice cream.
One campfire, one strawberry.
Gag, literally gag.
I like bath bombs, too.
You know, the big ones they always have in the baskets
near the entrance at specialty stores.
A little up-sell is fine.
Too bad that it wasn't enough to save Bed, Bath, and Beyond.
I like the bath bombs that fizzle with intensity.
I press the bomb deep,
like a battleship dropping a depth-charge.
A slow burn under water mine,
strategically armed and triggered
in the fleshy, vulnerable spot between my legs.
Fizzy bubbles pop and spurt on the water's surface,
like milk on a fresh bowl of Rice Crispies.
Hi, Kitty.
Mommy is ok.
Mommy just had to get some tears out, don't worry.
Come lay next to the tub beside Mommy.
Hundreds of tiny explosions down below,
deep below the churning surface where only
the submarine captain knows the truth.
Boom goes the first depth charge.
Gasp.

Boom goes the second depth charge.
Whimper.
I keep my thighs just barely apart
so the fizzy bubbles tickle between.
Let me tell you, this smut novel is helping
the battleship above find its mark below.
No, Kitty!
Kitty has jumped on the little table
and sent the candles tumbling to the floor.
Wax spatters the tile.
It will be a bitch to get wax out of the grout.
Let's be honest, I won't even try.
Both candles are extinguished by their own wax.
Isn't it funny that the fuel which keeps the flame
can also smother the flame?
Kitty slinks away and out the door,
leaving a small crack of light peeking into the bathroom.
I know what you are thinking,
but I only own one cat.
Don't worry about me,
I'm not a (crazy) cat lady.
Not yet.
I'm too relaxed to move.
In the faint crack of light,
I watch the two smoking wicks dance.
They dance alone and apart, but also together.
They are scared of each other,
but they are birds of the same feather.
You always know when you are of the same feather.
And the dark helps, obviously.
Dancing in the dark is safer.
You can hide your fear, hide your expressions, hide your tears,
hide your giggles when you feel his hard little pencil dick
battleship, accidentally pressing and docking against your belly.

The smoke is shy but spirited,
like my thighs with the fizzy bubbles between.
Fizzy love between salsa partners,
as the smoke slithers and slides around the dancing couple
lifting *up up up* and feeling drunk and stupid and in love.
I was in love with a boy once.
We danced in the dark once.
But he was a boy, and I was a girl.
Immature children in adult bodies.
One partner can be immature, but not both.
It was fun for a while, but we never had a real future.
He was a good battleship, he knew how to bomb me just right.
The candle wicks stop smoking.
The passion has burned out,
and the bath water is cold.
I reluctantly turn on the fluorescent lights and end my ritual.
I know they save the world or whatever,
but I really hate these new fluorescent bulbs.
The light isn't quite right.
The light feels fake,
the light feels like a flickering lie.
It's better than those horrible office building lights,
but not by much.
I will crack a window and let in some winter air
to clear the lingering, hanging, candle smoke.
It's funny how love sticks around like a heavy, black,
waxy cloud long after the love is over.
Even a mismatched love of campfire and strawberries,
bath bomb and fish market.

King of Rats

Free Verse with Internal Dialog

Three days ago, I had a panic attack.
I threw away everything I love,
I threw away all of my *addictions*.
Two days ago, I cried.
Yesterday, I pretended that I was feeling fine.
Today, I dug through the dumpster like a rat.
Salvaged pieces and parts of my life.
Wet, decay, rot, and rats.
There were only dead rats, I saw no signs of life.
Now my living room smells like trash,
but at least my withdrawals have been satiated.
Turn the music up, buy some beer.
Celebrate my trash life.
Crawl and scavenge amongst the bloated, bile-leaking rats.
Birds of a feather.

a bizarre form of hyper rationality
devoid of the typical ideological nonsense
or perhaps the episode was purely idealogical
a fish in a tank is just as ignorant to its own identity
as it is ignorant to the gravity of its situation
just as humans with gravity and telescopes
the gravity and functions of the chaotic universe
just fish in a fish bowl
with no concept of the outside world

i am the king of rats

From Below

Free Verse

Over the edge and into the hole.
My lips between your thighs,
Plunging tongue, French kiss.
Hold your breath, but the fall is too far.
Take one last breath, try try try...to inhale,
but you're going to drown.
Down here in the bleak,
in the wet hole.
Down here in the well,
not even the mold has the heart to fluer.
Flourish in the Vega supernova!

Cum for me, slut.

Your body is made of star dust,
the divine ribs of Adam.
A little breath of me.
Now you know what it feels like
under the water, under the surface tension.
Below the Starlight, below the water-treaders.
Bite their ankles from below.

Swallow it down,
nice and slow.

Question

Epistolary

if you scoured these pages
and found your name
hidden cryptically
would you blush with
heat and excitement
or would you flush with
frustration and anger?
if you opened my mind
and looked inside
would you be disappointed
if you couldn't find
a mention of yourself?

or would you be relieved?

Diarrhea of the Mouth

Free Verse

I try my best to be stoic
calm, cool, collected
I try to listen more than I speak
sometimes I don't speak at all
but when my heart gets involved
I turn into a blathering bimbo
hellbent on convincing you to like me
it's been so long since i last attempted small talk
i hate small talk
can't we just fuck?
in the same ways that I like you
I expose every nook and cranny of my brain
trying desperately to find something that you like about me
but it's only our second date
you never replied to half of my texts
but I won't bring it up
my heart turns me into puddle of teary mistakes
there is nothing left
the honeymoon phase is over before it even started
I didn't give you a chance to question yourself in my silence
didn't give you a chance to miss me
but then again, I never do
Gods knows, I suffered in your silence
it's so exhausting
giving everything up front
isn't it funny how giving too much pushes people away?

Bad Habit

Free Verse

i have a bad habit
of breaking my own heart
crush too hard
lust too intensely
love too quickly
it's convenient to blame the other person
to claim that they led me on
or lied to me
or cheated on me (*we weren't even official yet, she said*)
the scales of justice, like the sales of love
tilt in favor of truth and righteousness
if relationships were jury trials,
judged by peers
i would need jose baez
a successful compromise is when both parties are dissatisfied
it was a lovely first date
we talked for hours in the following days
and then i saw you holding hands with another
you broke my heart
no no wait, i must remember
that i broke my own heart
i am all heart, devoid of mind
a cup of blood overflowing with expectations
dissatisfaction is exclusively and delusionally mine
compromise between strangers is a fallacy
expectations are the assassins of second dates

Filth

Naked Poem

dirty girl
dirty bed
stinky girl
stinky sheets
fat and old
sad and cold
single and bored
boring and moody
childless but brooding
yellow toenails
clippings sail
filthy floor
barefoot whore
mold spore
plan b in the
middle drawer
broken mirror
bad-luck seer
self respect on the
drying rack
self-esteem on the
irony steam table
mental health on the
bottom shelf

Wet

Existential

i am in the kitchen bent over the counter
cooking, cleaning, humming a little song
the water supply hose breaks free from the washing machine
i fight the stream with both hands
but my face and chest are hopelessly drenched
the water pressure intensifies unnaturally
something is wrong
my children come running into the kitchen
their faces are the definition of panic
the water is so overwhelming that i cannot take a breath
i try to scream to the children to bring buckets
but my mouth is flooded and i cannot enunciate
my son bravely presses forward into the stream
and tries to give me a glass bowl
far too small, go get buckets
the sink faucet spontaneously bursts
before i can turn my head to look
water blasts from every wall
every cabinet
the kitchen is a torrential waterfall
an unnatural waterfall of impossibility
all i can do is scream
but i'm underwater and can't make a noise
the kitchen is filling up like a fish tank
i see my daughter and grab her
clutch her small body tightly to my chest
and as suddenly as this nightmare began
it stops
the water stops

the floor isn't even wet
i collapse to the floor and sit with my back against the cabinet
held tilted back, daughter still clutched tightly, both of us crying
i notice the cabinet beside me is open
i reach for the cabinet door to close it
my daughter coughs and my attention is diverted to her
my hand touches nothing
i look back to the open cabinet
it's closed
but i didn't close it
i get up and take my daughter's hand
we begin to move cautiously out of the kitchen
where is my son?
i haven't seen him since he offered the glass bowl
i take one step into the hallway and a
black mass blasts in front of me into the living room
one second later, my son appears from the living room
mommy, what's happening?
don't you worry about it, sweetheart
just stay with mommy
we stay together now
you don't even go to the bathroom alone
do you understand?
as i say this to him,
as i try to be brave an instill confidence and security,
i know it is a lie,
i know that i am powerless
the black mass rules me
has ruled me since i was old enough to dream
my first memories are nightmares
i shouldn't have brought children into this
i am powerless to shield my children
and i wonder if it even matters anymore
whatever this is

whatever has been following me my entire life
it is intensifying and growing stronger
becoming more bold, brazen, severe
it has begun to follow me to my friends' houses
windows shatter, fires start spontaneously
the guilt i feel for burdening others with this
this dead, black weight on my shoulders
it's like carrying around another person
except it's not a person at all
the strangest aspect is the brain pops
more like brain explosions
these are not long, thunder-like, rumbling, echoing explosions
have you ever heard a sonic boom?
that sharp crack that sounds like god clapped his hands
the shock wave and sound hit you hard
then it's over, just as quickly as it started
the brain explosions sound like that
i once read that this condition is known as
exploding head syndrome (ehs)
i'm fleeing my friend's house
the entity just behind me
causing more chaos than i could fit into these pages
or even attempt to explain
i am so sorry that i brought this upon my friends
CRACK
brain pop
(ehs)
i'm in a dark gray milieu
like a rainy winter dawn just before the sun rise
except there are no trees here
no ground under foot
no clouds
just that dark gray winter color
CRACK

brain pop
(ehs)
within the gray milieu, a black cloud forms
mostly opaque, but not completely
it swallows me whole and i know it is the entity
as the cloud billows and puffs around me
i catch glimpses of the gray, blank milieu
i try to scream out to someone, anyone
but no one can help me here
my voice is suffocated by the black cloud
CRACK
brain pop
(ehs)
i breathe deeply and, this time, the scream is loud
my eyes are wet
the yellow sun flutters through the window
alighting gently on my book shelf
my daughter and son lay sleeping next to me
all is calm
for now

\dating.exe\

Free Verse Couplets

I have become a husk of the lover I once proclaimed to be,
a cringy, distasteful claim made public at every inappropriate opportunity.

A backwards cocoon that contains not
a caterpillar struggling to grow and become a moth,
but a disease.
A virus poised to spread unpleasantries
to the brave few that have remained within my blast radius.

Someone once called me insufferable, and I laughed.
I still laugh, but now I laugh at how wrong I was.

Satin finished keyboard, the keys - fat and white,
the most obvious, the most boring, the most common.

Have you ever heard the sound of a creamy keyboard?
Like drops of lustful milk dripping into a thirsty pool of

STD's and single parents. "Not here for games or hookups."
What finally changed your mind?

I like games, I like hookups. Who doesn't like fun?
What you really mean to say is,

"I need help. Please rescue me."
Fun doesn't rescue people.

First responders always come last on the totem pole of attention,
despite being the invaluable sachem's head and footer.

They support the entire structure.
I'm not a misogynist; I'm a disgruntled libertine.

A slave without a Mistress; a schooner with a
spinning compass, bobbing in an ocean of doubt.

So I will wait in my cocoon and hope that the seasons pass
quickly enough that I die within my crumbling husk.

Reduce

Free Verse

I hate mirrors.
Always have, always will.
I'll be the first to admit that I suck at looking in the mirror,
both literally and figuratively.
I will say, however, that I am aware of the mirror,
both literally and figuratively,
and that is more than most people can say about themselves.
I am trying to reduce.
Isn't that what the girls say?
No, that is what they *used to say*.
The cosmopolitans.
The New Yorkers.
The socialites.
"I'm trying to reduce."
Not through weight loss, but through organ loss.
Let me ask you a question, reader.
Yes, you. I'm talking to you.
Have you read Sylvia Plath?
Please put down this book of mine and go read *The Bell Jar*.
The audiobook is also quite delicious.
Huge dollops of caviar and insane girls smoking cigarettes
in the same asylum that housed Ray Charles.
Be sure you find the audiobook with Maggie Gyllenhaal narrating.
Her voice will melt your brain and every part of your body.
The Bell Jar is my favorite book
and I think it will soon be your favorite.
Sylvia and I are reducing.
Will you join us in our reduction efforts?
How unfortunate that Ted Hughes did not reduce much sooner.

What a shit stain he was on humanity.
Fuck, Sylvia deserved better.
Please come join us in the oven.
Just put your head in the oven.
Follow the instructions.
Suicide is a recipe, you know?
Baking is a science
Just follow the instructions.
You will be fine.

I'm trying to reduce.

Homemade Whine

Free Verse

Some people are meant to struggle,
meant to wither on the grape vine.
Plucked with high hopes but turn out dry and fruitless.
No wine can come of these people.
Everything has been taken from them,
as a frozen spring morning shatters and destroys budding grapes.
The world is cold and relentless.
Perhaps a few grapes survive,
but the vines must run the gauntlet again next winter.
A vicious, repeating cycle of hope, failure, and despair.
Even in the most optimistic of years,
the fruits of their labors are smashed, fermented, and distilled.
Flesh turned to blood;
blood turned to profit;
profit turned to greed.
Even in the best years, your existence is dehumanized
and distilled down to usefulness and marketability.
Just let me be a dried, shriveled grape.
Let the frost take me, ravage my cells, and steal away my sweetness.
Allow me to savor my own bitterness,
as you rip me from the vine and toss me to the ground.
Heel on me, dear farmer.
Press me into the soil.
I will never be six feet deep, but I would accept six inches.
I'll be lucky to get one inch,
but I'll accept any attention your heel is willing to give.
Remember this anecdote, little grapes, and take solace:
regardless of how much the world strips away from you,
your grave is always waiting.

Even when you have nothing, you still have two things:
your attitude and your grave.
Greed cannot deny you a grave,
your friendly, comfortable, custom-fitted grave is waiting.
Underwhelming, underground, undertaker.
A shallow little grave for my shallow little life.
One shovel full of dirt at a time,
but not too quickly.
Or maybe just a boot kicking some dirt over my corpse.
Don't work yourself to death; there is no rush.
Busy work masquerading as action.

Smiling Through Pain

Free Verse

I am unable to smile through pain.
What do these heroic people have inside
that allows them to smile through pain?
Whatever it is, I don't have it.
I'm not talking about a stubbed toe or a paper cut.
I'm talking about deep, chronic, debilitating pain.
Pain that throbs with the beat of your heart.
Pain that prevents you from laying, sitting, sleeping, walking, driving.
My dad used to tell me stories about his sister.
About how she was never upset nor said a bad word about anyone
no matter how bad the cancer hurt.
Not even when the doctors took her legs.
She just kept right on snow skiing without legs.
Recently, I was violently told that I am struggling.
Yes, I struggle with pain and the suffocating
limitations it presses on my life,
but I am not a hero.
I cannot ski without legs.
I'm just a normal person.
So, yes. I struggle.
Is that what you wanted to hear?
The irony of a person who has been lucky enough to never
have a reason to struggle is explaining struggle
to a person who has only experienced brief flashes of happiness.
The irony is so intense that I must give up on you.

Haunted House

Free Verse with Internal Dialog

Can a house be haunted by failure?
Not a literal failure of the beams and walls,
although that is happening, too.
You know the old adage about a fly on the wall,
but what about the walls themselves?
Do they listen?

More importantly, do they remember?

Of all the house parts, maybe the walls
remember best of all.
I could show you several walls that remember
my fist and my boot,
a shovel and a slut or two,
a knife and a bullet (or two).

The black tar resin coating the hearth bricks.
Spider webs cling and dangle inside the fireplace
like the tomb of Cleopatra.

I would never throw a Queen against the wall, by the way.

The spiders don't like fire,
but their webs don't burn
and thus they accumulate year after year.
Night after cold night I sit by the fire and wallow in

failure
the failure to burn webs

or anything else, for that matter

I could clean the fireplace, clean the blackness,
clean the cobwebs out of my mind,
but what's the point?
It's not like anyone is going to be sitting here with me
to enjoy the new and improved view.
This is where the therapist steps in and says,
"But that's not the point of cleaning the fireplace.
You do that for yourself."
Well, I guess that's the problem.
The fireplace remembers that I am a failure,
and I like it that way because I can see it.
I like to keep an eye on the fireplace
so it can't sneak up on me.
Like a spider playing tricks.

Therapy is a narcissism machine operated by government-endorsed drug dealers.

The floor is collapsing.
It used to just be the kitchen,
now it is everywhere.
Below the floor, the house is sinking into the rot.
You might call it mud, but it isn't mud.
It's rot.
The floor is pretty, though.
Some of it, at least.
Not the bloody parts, but other areas look nice.
I leave the blood as a reminder not to be stupid.
Better yet, to remind me not to react to stupidity;
although, it could be argued that reacting to stupidity
is a greater sin than the initial, incendiary stupidity.
But I already said goodbye, said my piece/peace.
It was suggested to me that allowing dried,

chipping blood to remain on the floor is unsanitary.

Sometimes it is the dirty things that are the most healthy.

The dirty wall that isn't really dirty at all.
The ghostly remains of a fly trap caught in the breeze,
it swung around and slapped the wall.
Permanent stains of fly corpses.
Breezes that slips between the failing, single paned windows.
Glue strip stuck to the wall for weeks.
The wall has become a graveyard of wings and legs.
I don't recall reading on the fly trap packaging that the
glue is permanent and will become a part of your life.
I should probably concoct a lie about the dirty wall before
someone sees it, but there isn't anyone to see it.
"But that's not the point of cleaning the stain.
You do that for yourself."
Well, I guess that's the problem.

Someone really liked yellow.
My bathroom is yellow.
Not like a pleasant, vibrant, sunshine yellow
but a vomit, dirty, dehydrated urine yellow.
Floor tiles, back splash, shower surround, tub, paint,
wall paper, counter top, faucet.
Even the toilet is vomit yellow.
Yellow and stained with a century of hard water.
Stained with the shit splashed of my ostomy bag.
Splashed twenty times per day with shit,
and after a while stalagmites begin to form.
The toilet is beyond cleaning.
All I can do is use a flathead screw driver to chisel away
and try not to shatter the porcelain,
because then I will have to spend money on the nastiest room

I've ever seen in my life.
Honestly, it's the most disgusting room I have ever
seen in my entire life.
And it's mine.
All mine.
Did I mention that the counter is sinking into the crawlspace?
Did I mention that the sink leaks incessantly and
cultivates a colony of mold that rivals
even the colonies you can find under the house.

drip, drip, drip
dripping sink, dripping pipe
moldy cabinet
constant audible and olfactory reminder

reminder of failure and liberty

Voyeur in the Forest

Existential

There is a man in the forest.
He lurks amongst the thick undergrowth
behind my house.
On the brightest, most sunny days,
his blackness is pure.
A shadow, a silhouette, a void.
A void of all knowing and all watching
where information and happiness goes to die.
He watches me, and he documents my actions.
Like a war-time journalist reporting on horrendous and terrifying
war crimes that no one really wants to hear about or believe,
but you just can't look away from the talking head as it blathers on
like a low-budget slasher film.
I know the man in black isn't real,
the man in the forest isn't real.

I know.

"I know."
Fuck you, too.
He is just an obscure, grotesque, human-shaped statue,
but I cannot slough the irrational fear
which his constant, insistent, incessant presence evokes.
I peed outside this morning.
A gaping yawn, face to face with the pink and orange sunrise.
Steaming cup of fresh coffee in one hand, penis in the other hand.
The man in the forest was watching,
watching and documenting this alpha male routine.
The man in the forest has watched me for years,

but he never cared about my penis until today.
I probably should have felt naked, but rather,
I felt emboldened by the man's insistent gaze.
So I showed him my balls, too.
Balls really are the most repulsive aspect of human anatomy, aren't they?
Tell me what is more repulsive than balls.
He was impressed neither by my balls nor my penis.
I tried a florid little arabesque,
but he couldn't have cared less.

I must think of something I can do which would be worth
the effort of documenting, judging, and distributing.
(Does he use the Oxford comma, I wonder?)
Perhaps a particularly severe case of delirium tremens
would satiate the editor, who so diligently oversees and approves
(or rejects)
the various journalistic endeavors of the man in the forest.

Finish

Eulogy

"Life is not a race."
A popular piece of advice.
The problem with this advice,
is that it is only one side of the coin.
I will submit that life is not a race in the following way:
your life is not a race against society.
Your life is not a race against other people.
I absolutely will accept this as true.
"Life is not a race."
But here lies the issue, dear reader:
this advice applies objectively to comparisons.
"Life is not a race" becomes problematic when we examine the individual.
The individual,
their merits,
their dreams,
their goals,
their achievements,
their accomplishments,
their reputation,
their attitude.
In terms of the individual,
life is absolutely a race,
but who does the individual race against?
If not other people,
if not society,
then who is the opponent?
The opponent is Death.
Believe me when I tell you,
no human can outrun Death.

The individual race we run has only one winner.
Death.
Undefeated for all eternity.
The race of the individual is more of a treadmill.
The exercise of running in place.
Yes, this is a doomed race,
but fear not!
There is hope!
You cannot win the race against Death,
but you can give him one hell of a run for His money.
Don't pay the Boat Man just yet.
This is what you must do, dear reader:
you cannot alter your race with Death,
but you can start a new race.
A race against yourself.
Finish everything you start.
All of your work, your dreams, your family, and your desires.
Finish everything that makes you happy.
Get on that treadmill and sprint until you can't breathe.
Until your sweat drips from every pore.
Finish your races.
You cannot win against Death,
but you can win victories along the way for yourself.
On the home stretch,
stuck in a hospital bed.
No one brings their goals and dreams to the ICU.
No one finishes their dreams in the ICU.
Death wins.
Death finishes.

Death is catching up!

Finish what you started.

The End

www.ingramcontent.com/pod-product-compliance
Lightning Source LLC
LaVergne TN
LVHW010644110826
845149LV00014B/2945